LEAD LIKE A
KING/QUEEN

LEAD LIKE A KING/QUEEN

Leadership Principles from
the Judean Kings/Queen

Charles H. Gaulden

Samuel S. Hemby

gatekeeper press™

Columbus, Ohio

Lead Like a King/Queen: Leadership Principles from the Judean Kings/Queen

Published by Gatekeeper Press
2167 Stringtown Rd, Suite 109
Columbus, OH 43123-2989
www.GatekeeperPress.com

Library of Congress Control Number: 2021934982

ISBN (paperback): 9781662911835
eISBN: 9781662911842

Dedication

"To my wife, Rita, the greatest life-mate one could ever dream for. Thank you, "sweetness," for the many years of constant support, encouragement, and partnership you have provided. Your soft words of inspiration have, so many times, been the catalyst to keep going when the "it's not worth it" walls appeared. This book was certainly no exception! I love and appreciate you more than can be expressed." - Sam Hemby.

"To my wife, Vanessa, the love of my life. What a great wife, friend, and support you have been to me in all things. Each day is a joy to be with you!" – Charles Gaulden

Table of Contents

Foreword

Lead! You may be in a critical leadership position now, or you may envision leading in the future. Some people are born to lead and know it from the time they leave the crib. Others unexpectedly find themselves thrust into a place where others are looking to them as example.

Whatever the case may be, you have picked up an incredible resource to empower you to lead in the best way possible. Throughout human history, leaders have charted the course for nations, organizations, and churches. There is no such thing as a perfect leader – we can all improve – and if we want to be the best leaders we can be, we need to know the right ways to lead.

The Holy Bible has always served as the source of authority and guidance for God's people. It is filled with both positive and negative examples for leaders seeking to lead God's way. One of the best places to turn to learn how to teach is in the lives of the kings of the Kingdom of Judah.

My friends and colleagues, Doctors Charles Gaulden, and Sam Hemby, are uniquely qualified to help us distill timeless leadership lessons from these kings' stories. Both are outstanding professors who teach all students at Southeastern University (SEU), one of the largest Christian universities in North America. They both excel in teaching new, first-year students and megachurch pastors in their doctoral programs.

Charles pastored one of the largest churches in South Carolina before becoming Professor of Old Testament for us at SEU. He has an incredible gift for taking his in-depth knowledge of the Old Testament Hebrew text, the historical setting of the Old Testament, and the latest archeological findings to make the Old Testament message relevant and unforgettable for all of his students. He is finishing his second doctorate after completing two master's degrees beyond the Doctor of Ministry and Master of Theology he earned at Erskine Seminary and the Master of Philosophy he earned at the University of Bangor United Kingdom. You will find his insights from the biblical account of the Judean kings to be fascinating and profound, as well as relevant for any leadership application today.

Sam earned his Ph.D. in Organizational Leadership from Regent University School of Entrepreneurship and Leadership" after earning an MA from Trinity Evangelical Divinity School and pastoring churches across the country. He has been teaching at Southeastern University for twenty years, spending most of those developing and leading our graduate studies department and degree programs. His contribution to this book will explore the biblical principles we can learn from the kings of Judah and show how they can work today. He provides many real-world examples to drive home these vital lessons. Reading with both of these incredible men of God gives you a chance to journey through two worlds as you will see biblical principles come alive in ways you can integrate into your leadership.

I encourage you to grab your Bible and follow along with the biblical text as you discover how these ancient leaders' timeless examples can help you lead in the best way possible. Be ready to examine your mindset and practices to make the changes necessary to avoid the costly mistakes too many of these kings made and see the successes of the best of them.

Alan Ehler, D.Min
Dean, Barnett College of Ministry and Theology and Professor of Practical Theology,
Southeastern University, Lakeland, Florida
Author of *How to Make Big Decisions Wisely* (Zondervan, 2020)

Chapter One – Kings Rehoboam (931-913) and Abijah (913-911) 1 Kings 12-15; 2 Chronicles 10-13

The coronation for King Rehoboam had finally arrived. His famous father, King Solomon, had died and the nation had shown their respects to him at his recent funeral. The customary grieving period had passed, and the coronation for the new king would be held at Shechem in the northern portion of Israel. Shechem means "shoulders" in Hebrew, as the rock formation of the local mountain range gave the appearance of two strong, adjacent shoulders.

1. What King Rehoboam Did Right at His Coronation

In the past, Shechem had a long and memorable history for the Jewish nation. Abraham, Isaac, and Jacob had journeyed in this region. Jacob's well was still nearby — and exists even to our time. Joshua had erected a large memorial stone that partially remains to this day, as does Joseph's tomb. As well-developed shoulders can be a symbol of strength and balance, so was this location in the minds of the people. The choice of Shechem for the coronation ceremony was historically wise.

For Rehoboam's present, additional political rationale was important for his coronation at Shechem rather than in the capital city of Jerusalem. The northern tribes of the nation had legitimate concerns with the way Solomon had taxed them heavily for many years. He often used the bulk of the funds with his own home tribe, the southern tribe of Judah. Talk of nepotism constantly abounded and strong resentment prevailed. The northern tribes frequently felt neglected in the priority list of the leadership. For them, Solomon's priorities revealed his values and they felt undervalued by the southern leadership. Thus, the northern Shechem choice was also politically wise.

Additionally, Solomon used a very unpopular conscription method of requiring all able-bodied males to serve for 1 to 2 months per year in difficult, manual building projects. The males often were away from their families during those periods. To add salt to the wounds, they were harshly treated by receiving poor wages and living conditions, and even beatings. In an economy that was virtually all agrarian, the absence of fathers and sons was a great hardship on the women and children. Even the Persian king, Cyrus, criticized the Babylonians for the use of conscription (also called corvée).[1] The bitterness ran deep in the north. Therefore, the Shechem location was also sociologically wise.

So far so good. Rehoboam and his leaders wisely chose the right location and calmly listened to the concerns of the people. The king correctly requested three days to consider the people's proposal. The win/win offer of the people was an extraordinarily generous offer. They were willing to serve King Rehoboam with the same respect and loyalty as they had given to his father Solomon for 40 years. They only appealed for reasonable adjustments with taxes and conscription.

First, Rehoboam wisely requested the counsel of the older men who had served his father faithfully for 40 years. In essence, they said, "This is a great deal. Simply speak kindly to your people and yield to these reasonable requests." One would think that such wise counsel ended the meeting, and the king would speak kindly to his people, and the positive fruit of the decision would be long-lasting.

2. What King Rehoboam Did Wrong at His Coronation

Unfortunately, Rehoboam also listened to the counsel of his friends whom he knew from his childhood years. They took an opposite approach, suggesting that he demonstrate himself to be much stronger than his father. Say, "My little finger is stronger than my father's waste." They also added this admonition: say, "My father beat you with whips, but I will beat you with scorpions." (A scorpion whip wove pieces of bone, iron, or wood into the leather straps.) This advice could not have been worse.

Unbelievably, Rehoboam chose the foolish counsel of his childhood friends. "How dumb could one be and still breathe oxygen?" is the obvious question. The people were aghast. They saw no win/win scenario. Instead, only an immature king would win, and they would lose big time.

The arrogant and out-of-touch king sent his official, Hadoniram, his father's labor leader, to enforce the regal orders as before. However, the people not only refused the official's orders but stoned Hadoniram to death. Stoning was a capital judgment usually reserved for murderers and other high crimes. The rash, insolent king's boasting ended, and he fled to Jerusalem, barely escaping with his own life.

The northern tribes responded in the same way as Rehoboam had so rudely sown. He reaped the biggest lose/lose imaginable. He had threatened to use a scorpion whip, and now the people had acquired their own type of scorpion whip. They beat him with a painful, national split. Ten of the twelve tribes left and formed their own country. They even kept the original name of Israel. He was left with his family's tribe of Judah, and the small tribe of Benjamin. The political division between Israel and Judah would last for well over two centuries. However, numerous negative effects of the national divorce would endure even to the time of Christ, more than nine centuries later.

In the first few days of his reign, the new king had managed to lose more than 80 percent of his nation. Solomon's beginning reign was marked by a wise moment and knotty judicial decision when he shrewdly recommended the splitting of a baby in half to discover the child's true mother. His wisdom united his nation behind him (1 Kings 3). "Splitting the baby" has even survived to our judicial lexicon today for "tough judicial decisions."

The beginning of Rehoboam's reign was marked by a foolish moment of splitting an entire nation. Though Rehoboam means "enlarger," he had become a "shrinker" overnight. Perhaps "a

Rehoboam" expression should also survive to our personal lexicon for "terrible decisions." Once we make a decision, the decision makes us.

Hints exists that Solomon had misgivings about his son (Eccl. 2, 4). Later, even Rehoboam's own son, King Abijah, described his father's beginning at this point as "young, inexperienced, and weak." Rehoboam was like a plant grown in the shade, that never reached full growth. He had only known luxury, isolation from real people's problems, and zero experience in leading. He seemed to have "maturity arrestation," with a level closer to one in his early teenage years rather than a 41-year-old. Sadly, his friends were also on the same novice level. This is proof that friendships are like water and seek their own level.

3. What King Rehoboam Did Right After His Coronation

Rehoboam's foolishness was rooted in his arrogance. The same arrogance that forsook wise counsel, abandoned reasonableness, and rebuffed people's goodwill offer with harsh threats was still present with his character. The resulting fruit on the tree was anger. Rather than face himself, he shifted blame to the northern tribes, whom he saw as needing punishment. A bloody civil war in the Jewish land lay a hair trigger away. Rehoboam adopted the same mindset as the ancient Pharaoh of the exodus, who over-calculated the superiority of his army against the newly freed Hebrew slaves.

Into our biblical narrative, a venerated prophet is introduced named Shemaiah. He arrives with a strong word. His delivery was succinct, "This is what the Lord says: Do not fight against your brothers, the Israelites. Go home, every one of you, for this is my doing." Shemaiah's message intersected with the time aspects of past, present, and future.

As to the past, the prophet Ahijah the Shilonite had previously prophesied during the days of Solomon that the nation would split.

The past message of Ahijah was grounded in a rebuke of Solomon's wayward and abusive policies. Solomon had sown the seeds of disunity for years. Now, the Solomonic harvest ripened on his son's coronation day. The prophesying of Ahijah was now fulfilled.

As to the present, Shemaiah intercepted another possible foolish decision by the king. To Rehoboam's credit, he did accept the prophetic admonition of the respected prophet. The king called off the invasion. The intervention prevented a bloody civil war between Rehoboam and the new northern king, Jeroboam.

As to the future, Shemaiah's prophetic word addressed both northern and southern tribal areas to focus on their common heritage and act civil toward each other. Unfortunately, both sides would challenge this prophetic counsel. Tensions remained all the years of the reigns of Rehoboam and Jeroboam.

A bright moment now appears in our narrative. Rehoboam finally learned some valuable lessons. He had painfully attended "I Messed Up University." Reality hit him. He never received training for his role as king. Equally, he was keenly aware of the lurking danger of the ambitious King Jeroboam. Rehoboam adjusted quickly with a two-pronged approach that would mark the next three years of his leadership. The text states that he acted wisely.

First, he would give his sons needed leadership training. Each son was assigned a responsibility with accountability. This decision kept his family in the trenches with his people's concerns. This time he would truly listen to his people and quickly address their concerns. The move established peace in his land. He wisely surveyed his sons' performance and chose his successor with the best leadership qualities, instead of the traditional first-born method.

The second approach dealt with the border cities to Judah's east, west, and south. Real dangers had emerged from the surrounding nations, even in the later years of his father's reign. He would not get caught unprepared; therefore, he embarked on a major refortification campaign. In recent years, archaeologists have uncovered refortification projects dating to Rehoboam's time period.[2]

Finally, the Judean king knew that his northern neighbor, King Jeroboam, was an untrustworthy man. The north already had a larger population. It would not be long before Jeroboam would be able to fully equip a standing army. Rehoboam had wisely left the northern border between Israel and Judah relatively open, as many people visited the temple in Jerusalem during special events. However, Rehoboam diligently prepared the nation for the possibility of major conflicts arising between north and south. His son, Abijah, would inherit this wise preparation.

4. What King Rehoboam Did Wrong After His Coronation

Even hard-learned lessons can be forgotten during prosperous times. In his fourth year, after being firmly established and strong, King Rehoboam and his leadership team abandoned the commandments of the Lord. They participated in idolatry, and in so doing, his unfaithfulness dropped the divine protective hedge around his nation.

The prophet Shemaiah once again appeared before King Rehoboam. The summary of his first visit had been "Do not go." His second visit's message was "Egypt will come." The piercing message had its desired effect. The king and his leadership team humbled themselves and acknowledged the justice of God.

Pharaoh Shishak (also known as Shoshek I in one of his variant Egyptian forms) invaded Judah at this time. Pharaoh Shoshek I records his invasion of Judah in amazing detail in the Bubastite Portal of Karnak.[3] The Judean nation would be spared, but not without major tribute to Egypt. Vast treasure from both palace and temple went to Egypt. The famous Solomonic gold shields, used for pageantry celebrations, vanished. Rehoboam replaced them with inferior bronze shields. The inferiority between Solomon's reign and the later Judean kings would last for three and a half centuries.

5. What King Abijah (Abijam) Did Right During His Reign.

King Abijah only ruled for three years. As stated earlier, he was not king Rehoboam's firstborn son, so he did not acquire kingship due to birthright. Rather, he had most likely been chosen due to his leadership training. His leadership abilities had been beaten out on the anvil of real life. He had stood out among his brothers, and his father recognized the leadership qualities in him. The preparatory training his father instituted had paid off.

Early in his reign, King Jeroboam approached King Abijah with an army twice his size. Rather than fleeing, King Abijah boldly confronted the larger foe. He confronted the blatant idolatry instituted by Jeroboam along with his bogus priesthood.

The battle ensued with Jeroboam's superior numbers almost winning the day. However, the scribes recorded King Abijah and his army crying out to God. Their prayers were heard. Not only was Judah's defeat averted, but Jeroboam's army was crushed. Jeroboam died shortly afterwards, and the land had peace for 10 years.

Conclusion on King Rehoboam and King Abijah

The prophets Shemaiah and Iddo kept written records of these times, portions of which are preserved in the biblical text. Rehoboam's 17-year reign ended with a prophetic portrait of his leadership. Yes, he had done wrong by yielding to idol worship. Yet, the text at the end of his reign highlights his mother's Ammonite heritage. In so doing, the record may be offering a root, negative influence on Rehoboam. The Ammonites as a whole were strongly rooted in idolatry and child sacrifice. Had his mother imparted some of the Ammonite ways to her son?

The author of 2 Kings uses king Abijah's more secular name Abijam (father – sea) rather than his religious name Abijah (father –

Yahweh), perhaps to distinguish him from Jeroboam's son who also was named Abijah. The narrative in 2 Kings gives some negative information about the king. He served the Lord, but not with a whole heart. The author of 2 Chronicles focuses solely on the good in Abijah.

Which account is correct? The answer is both. From a certain viewpoint, we will see terrible qualities in these Judean kings. At other junctures, we see good arise. The prophetic portraits reveal both sides. King Abijah did not always serve God fully. Nevertheless, he did exercise courage, confront overwhelming odds, and prayed. Though he reigned only three years, he delivered Judah from certain destruction. He played an important role in the Davidic dynasty, which continued for centuries.

In spite of the negative reports about king Rehoboam, we are also left with a reminder of his humbling himself. God had mercy on king and country alike. He had been foolish, however, he regrouped and made wiser decisions. Yes, both he and his nation had been disciplined, but they were not destroyed. The prophetic portrait states, "Indeed there was some good in Judah."

Application: Chapter 1 - Rehoboam - Counterfeit Collaboration

It was definitely not my finest hour. Pastoring a small church while completing a graduate-level degree was both an exciting opportunity as well as a genuine challenge. As the church began to show some growth, particularly in the areas of youth and young adults, the leader, who was not a "rookie," was setting the stage for what was to be a rookie-like mistake!

Growth in the arena mentioned above brought about the need to navigate the process of hiring another staff member to work primarily in the youth department. Discussions were lively and positive as meetings to move forward with the new hire yielded strong affirmation and were approved by the appropriate congregational entities. It was exciting for all as potential candidates submitted fresh resumes and staff conducted initial phone interviews. After several weeks, a prime candidate had emerged from the search. As lead pastor of this congregation, I felt quite strongly about the need to secure the "prime candidate" and shared that with several of the leadership team within the church structure, my intent to hire this individual.

However, the campaign contained a critical omission. I neglected to allow a significant voice from a special couple into the conversation. This couple had been very faithful as volunteers of their time and energies to lead the youth ministry but was, for the most part, overlooked in the decision at hand. Realizing this family's voice should have had more consideration, I called the husband (we will call him John) into a meeting one evening, supposedly to get his opinion on the potential candidate. We began that meeting by discussing some of the youth endeavor's responsibilities and then I brought up the candidate under consideration. "What do you think?" was my simple question to John. His answer stunned me and, to this day many years later, still causes me to shudder: "You want to know what I think? Here's what I think. I don't think you care what I think because I think you already have your mind made up and it doesn't make any difference what I think!"

John's comments nailed me to the wall and called me out on something very dangerous in leadership context, something I have come to label *counterfeit collaboration*. Counterfeit collaboration is present when a leader acts as though they want to hear the perspectives of others and to involve them in the decision-making and execution of plans but, in actuality, they have already determined the course of action; they are only feigning interest in the opinion of other organizational constituents. Suffice it to say, my situation with John and his family did not end well (the congregation lost several good families as a result). If you have ever been guilty of this "rookie mistake," your endeavor was most likely quite unfruitful as well.

Rehoboam experienced the very negative impact counterfeit collaboration can have on a large-scale, national level! While present-day leaders can certainly draw many applications from this discussion, two areas, assigned versus emergent leadership and a multi-generation appreciation, are of particular import.

Assigned vs. Emergent Leadership

Leadership research has included quite a bit of conversation over the last few years concerning the difference in assigned leadership and emergent leadership. Assigned leadership is essentially influence exercised out of the base of position and title. Authority from the assigned position is understood as a part of the institutional culture and is a legitimate exercise of power by organizational constituents. On the other hand, Emergent leadership is influence based, not on position or title, but rather on permission given from a group as a leader "emerges" through more interactive and relational means. Both leadership types have a place in the effective function and productivity of a team setting and work in tandem to accomplish set organizational goals.

However, while much of the literature tends to treat these two types of leaders as two separate tracks upon which the organizational train travels, more thought and corresponding practice in this regard need consideration for 21st century leadership. More recent trends have caused assigned leadership influence to be much more short-lived (positional power via title has a very short shelf life compared to previous generations) and thus catapulted the need to emphasize attaining and maintaining leadership impact from a more emergent approach.

We have reached a day when all leaders, even those with formal positions and authority, must recognize the need to intentionally move into an arena of influence based on emergent leaders' characteristics. In other words, once a leader is appointed to a position, that person would be well-served to begin to picture their influence as an hourglass that has been turned over with the sand swiftly running out. The grains of positional influence will soon run out, and, in the meantime, relational influence from the permission granted by constituents will need to be in the process of development. In other words, leaders that will be effective in present-day organizational contexts will have to lead from both tracks, even when endowed with a title! Rehoboam could have profited greatly from this understanding!

While several components comprise emergent leadership, including the strong commitment to being interactive, relational, and communicative, one of the primary characteristics is always listening with a genuine concern and empathetic ear. Followers (volunteers or paid staff) in any contemporary setting are going to prove true the well-worn maxim, "People do not care what you know until they know that you care." Inaugurated as the new king of Israel, Rehoboam became the recipient of a position infused with much leadership authority. However, the people's request to slightly lighten the load that his father had imposed was a request that smacked of the desire for a more caring style of listening and authentic concern. With just a little relational intelligence, Rehoboam could have created a strong "culture of servanthood" ("if you serve them, they will serve you forever" – 1 Kings 12:7) and may have been a great example of someone whose position benefited all constituents. Unfortunately, the KING refused to listen and created one of the most horrendous leadership debacles in history.

One other issue needs mentioning here. I can almost hear someone saying, "Hey, Rehoboam did have a listening ear. He listened to his peers and followed their advice." On the surface, this is true. At a deeper, more leadership-centric level, though, this is partial "deafness" caused by selective listening (hearing only what you want to hear) and probably the façade of counterfeit collaboration we discussed earlier (remember John?). For whatever reason, Rehoboam's destructive actions based on horrible advice also highlights the need for another tool in the 21st-century leader's belt: a multi-generation appreciation.

Multi-generation Appreciation

The practice of selective listening (a first cousin to counterfeit collaboration!) is characterized by collecting information from various sources but with a predetermined mindset of only giving true credence to a select group. Rehoboam is a case in point. He gathered information from many but chose only to act on the radical advice received from a group of long-time peers. This practice is foolish at best and can be very dangerous and ultimately quite counter-productive, as Rehoboam's example certainly proves to be. Leaders who attempt to function from the limited scope of information, including a uni-generational perspective, often find themselves missing valuable and sometimes institutionally fatal insights.

The fact is that God will often choose to use very unlikely sources (in our preconceived notions) to bring some powerful and much-needed direction and provision. His grace extends to us in this fashion as He keeps us sensitive and guards us against becoming victims of self-induced tunnel-vision!

A Lesson from Bill

Many years ago, I served as a staff pastor with a lead pastor who had previously served a church that experienced significant growth and thus found it necessary to purchase additional property to expand. I will never forget the story he shared with me one day regarding fundraising for this endeavor. Having gathered in an open forum any interested congregational constituents, this leader and the people began to brainstorm potential ideas about raising money to purchase the new property. Among the meeting participants was a gentleman (let's call him Bill) who was a faithful church member. Bill was known by most everyone who had attended the church for any length of time because of his faithful attendance, welcoming demeanor, and overall great personality. However, there was an issue with Bill... everyone knew that he was not only faithful, friendly, etc., but Bill was also "not quite all there." Though chronologically much older, Bill had only the mental capacity of someone much younger (perhaps early teens). In common vernacular, "Bill's a great guy, but he's a little 'off'."

As my pastor friend was taking ideas from the floor, many suggestions were being made as to how best to connect with family and friends to raise funds needed. As the meeting was winding down, you guessed it... Bill stood up to offer his suggestion. He proposed without hesitation, "I think we should ask all the Hollywood movie-stars for some money to help us buy this property and build this church." There were several moments of silence as people politely smiled while also casting glances at each other that said, "that's surely a goofy idea, but we love Bill and, after all, this can be expected from him because he's not quite 'all there.'" Fortunately, a wise and loving pastor smiled and thanked Bill for his contribution to the conversation and then closed the discussion.

A few weeks later, the post office notified the Pastor to pick up a certified mail piece. When arriving at the post office and receiving the letter, it was with disbelief that my friend opened the envelope and found a nice note and a cashier's check for $5000.00 from Frank Sinatra! In the early 1980s, one should note that $5000 would be worth approximately $17,000 in 2021 (www.dollartimes.com). After gathering his composure and verifying the check's validity, the church then set out to find out how Frank Sinatra's organization got word of the need from a small church in a relatively small city some 3000 miles away. You guessed it... Bill!

As it turns out, Bill took it upon himself to buy one of the "celebrity newspapers" while standing in line at the grocery checkout. He found information in it, including addresses to use if one wanted to contact a particular star. He had personally written and sent a fundraising letter to many of those addresses, and much to everyone's total surprise, Frank Sinatra received it and responded!

Never underestimate a person or group of people God may place in your path to bring some "right on time" counsel!

Information Explosion

The amount and accessibility of information in our society over the last few decades have surely changed the world in many ways, some good, some not so much. Two expectations created by the information explosion are of particular import to leaders in the counterfeit collaboration conversation.

First, better-informed people have a more intense desire to be included in a more participative structure to speak into decision-making processes and plans. A well-worn but still relevant communication mantra reminds us, "Informed people are happy people." This reminder that most have heard often helps the leader recognize the sense of satisfaction and empowerment that can permeate an organizational culture when constituents believe the leadership is sharing up-to-date and appropriate information. Not to do so is to create a climate of suspicion that quickly erodes the vital foundation of trust.

Twenty-first-century leadership understands that it is both an informed people and an informing people that are happy people! It is certainly true that if leaders are to expect buy-in, they must be willing to allow input!

The second and perhaps a little less obvious fruit created by the information explosion is the expectation of intentional diversity within the leadership team and speaking into important organizational issues. However, one should not perceive this expectation's motive as a strong-handed move to dilute or divert legitimate processes. The diversity is more of a desperate cry for safe and well-rounded insights that speak into processes that connect present practices to a proud past while providing potential traction for a desired future! One thing the proliferation of information has done is it has provided a glance into how much we do not know! Recognizing gaps in knowledge has made upcoming generations potentially more open to and appreciative of those who "know what we don't."

I recently conducted an informal survey among graduating seniors from baccalaureate programs at the Christ-centered university where I teach. Most of these were either immediately pursuing vocational positions in local churches or non-profit ministry contexts or eventually doing so. To determine some of the most important expectations of this group of "recruits" related to places they desire to worship and work, I pursued several open-ended questions with the participants. One revealing response received from this group was especially surprising and encouraging.

When asked about planting new churches or starting new ministries within the church, the group was unanimous about the desire to have multiple generations involved in the new ministry's foundation and ongoing operation. Though the majority of those in this survey session were from Gen Z (born @1995-2015), not one person voiced the desire to start a "church for us," a "church for millennials," or even a "church for older people." While they shared the desire and expectation to have a genuine voice in the context, this group overwhelming agreed with the following compiled paraphrase of several actual comments:

> I do not want to work on a team where it's just a bunch of young people talking. We need to have a say but not the only say. We have come to realize and appreciate the fact that those who have gone before us have "gold" to share that we could never mine without their presence and participation. We are looking to pour our energies into a place that models and is led by people who celebrate a multi-generational, gender-inclusive, multi-ethnic, and society-impacting approach to ministry. We have seen too many begin and then fail because the culture was too exclusive and the information base too narrow. Hopefully, while we have much to learn, we have learned the lesson that we all need everyone else.

May there be a genuine welcome extended to a new generation of leaders who will genuinely collaborate and listen to others! May the ears of these leaders be open to diverse peoples and perspectives. May they discern in the listening the real direction of God, and may they correspondingly move the church, nation, and world forward with the courage and resolve necessary to hear the much anticipated "Well Done" (Matt. 25).

Chapter Two – King Asa (911-870) 1 Kings 15; 2 Chronicles 14-16

1. He Began Well

King Asa proved to be one of the best kings Judah ever produced. He ruled for 41 years. Most of those years he led with courage, foresight, preparation, and tremendous zeal for what was right. Many good qualities of leadership can be found in Asa, particularly at the beginning of his reign.

The young king fervently maintained the traditional worship of Yahweh. He rooted out idolatry at every opportunity. He removed the images, altars, high places, and groves of the idols. His reforming manifested also with informing. Simultaneously, through the idolatrous purging, he also informed the nation on how to keep the commandments. The right things also needed to replace the wrong things, and Asa made sure this process happened.

His leadership not only revealed itself in what he tore down, but also in what he built up. The land had an extended period of rest from war. Rather than sit back and fall into a lull, Asa wisely challenged his people to make the most of the peacetime. He refortified city walls, towers, and gates. His actions protected his nation and prepared them for what would become their greatest military trial and victory.

Egypt kept Judah under submission and tribute for many years since the initial invasion by Pharaoh Shishak. A contractual peace existed between the two nations, but only if Judah remained subservient. After King Asa's 10 years of peace and preparation, once again a major war arose from the twenty-second dynasty of Egypt. Did Asa stop the imposed tribute and thus triggered the invasion, or was it pure greed on Egypt's part for more plunder? We do not know the catalyst, but we do know that King Asa demonstrated remarkable leadership during the battle.

The record does not state whether the invaders' leader, named Zerah, was a pharaoh or a general of the army. The Pharaoh at this time was named Osorkon and an Ethiopian ruler was named Azerch. Both names could be phonetically carried over into Hebrew as Zerah. The region of Cush/Ethiopia was under Egyptian control at this time.[4] The invaders outnumbered Judah at least two to one.

Against all odds, Asa honored God, fought hard, and led his army well. In fact, the smaller Judean force soundly defeated the enemy by pursuing them all the way to the coastal plain of Gerar. Asa's victorious troops returned with a staggering amount of plunder. Egypt's mindset toward Judah changed. The Egyptian incursions into Judah ceased until the time of King Josiah, some three centuries later.

Into the victory celebrations, the prophet Azariah, son of Oded, exhorted the victorious king and troops. The prophet reminded them of past histories when the nation won military victories but quickly regressed rather than remaining vigilant. "Learn from the past," was the prophetic portrait in leadership. Now they must battle natural apathy, which often follows hard-fought battles.

Both the king and the people rose to the occasion and renewed their covenant with utmost sincerity. A national resurgence of good swept through the land. For example, King Asa deposed his grandmother Maacah (Hebrew uses the same word for mother and grandmother). She had made a repulsive image for the worship of Asherah, which was frequently accompanied with immoral acts and even child sacrifice.

After these needed reforms were completed, he instituted a great feast in Jerusalem at Solomon's temple. The northern kingdom had experienced internal conflict after the fall of Jeroboam I's short dynasty. However, Asa's Judean kingdom enjoyed the fruit of good leadership and God's blessings. Therefore, many Jews from the northern kingdom migrated to Judah. Nearly four decades earlier, the two kingdoms split. What a contrast the two were now in such a short time.

2. He Ended Weak

Two events in the latter reign of Asa tarnished his leadership history. In the previous Egyptian conflict, Asa had bravely faced a superior army and led his nation to victory. Now he would overestimate the enemy's strength, while diminishing the Lord's strength. In so doing, he set the nation up for future challenges with their neighboring country, Syria.

The scribe lists the thirty-sixth year as an important date in the chronology. The 36 years echo back to the start of the division of the nation of Israel into two nations, rather than the actual years of Asa's reign. Why is this method of dating inserted at this point? The reason may be to emphasize how dangerous this northern Israel invasion was to the Judean kingdom. Without intervention, Judah could well cease to exist after a mere 36 years as a nation.

King Baasha of Israel most likely confronted King Asa of Judah with superior numbers. Rather than boldly face Baasha as he had faced Zerah years earlier, he chose to form an alliance with Ben-Hadad I, the king of Aram/Damascus/Syria (all three names are interchangeable in the Bible for Israel's bordering neighbor).[5] Asa employed a monetary bribe to Ben-Hadad. Asa convinced him to break his treaty with King Baasha and invade Israel.

The plan worked as Asa had hoped. He managed to divert Baasha without a battle. It only cost him treasures from the temple and his palace. At least, this is all he could see the venture costing him. Little did he realize that he set in motion a negative legacy. Syria would be emboldened and become a thorn in the Jewish people's side for decades.

The prophet Hanani confronted Asa for his dependence on the Syrian king. Instead, Asa should have trusted God, and the king would have experienced a present victory akin to his past victory. Though the word was corrective, the essence of the prophetic portrait spoke to Asa's potential. He should not have overestimated the strength of his enemy, nor underestimated what he could have accomplished. Rather than heed the stinging message, he angrily threw Hanani into prison. Asa also brutally oppressed some of his people at this time. We are not told the reason for the people's oppression, but we can assume they had sided with Hanani.

King Asa's reaction with Baasha is completely opposite of the bold actions he took against Zerah years earlier. Why the sudden change? A clue is found in the book of Jeremiah, which was amazingly given 300 years after these events. In Jer. 41:9, the prophet makes a comment on an existing cistern to his day with, "Asa the king had made it for fear of Baasha king of Israel." The root was fear. Perhaps due to so much fortification work done to his eastern, western, and southern borders— but little with the northern one — left Judah open to attack from the northern kingdom of Israel. Fear gripped Asa and affected his calculations.

In the last two years of Asa's reign, he was afflicted with a severe foot disease. Numerous physicians have speculated possible conditions such as gout, diabetes, etc. We do not know the specific details of the disease, but only that the pronounced elements were in the feet. During this two-year span, he sought only the physicians and not the Lord. A subtle hint appears that he again underestimated the potential of the Lord's help in the midst of great negative situations. God was willing to work with his healing process if the king had only sought the Lord.

Conclusion on King Asa

After his reign of 41 years, King Asa died. The people greatly honored him in his death with a major funeral. Most of the Judean kings were buried in the royal tombs, but Asa had requested a tomb be cut out for himself in the city of David. The special tomb construction may indicate his desire to leave a lasting legacy. He did leave a positive legacy at the beginning of his reign when he sought God fully. He also bravely confronted an invading army. His actions kept Egypt away from invasion for centuries. Nevertheless, his trust faded at the end of his reign, causing that part of his legacy to be seen negatively. The scribes may hint at this with the expression, "the events of his reign from beginning to end." Beginning well is indeed important, but ending well is also important. The ultimate legacy is to strive for both.

Application - Chapter 2 - Asa - The Peril of Success

As I write today, I am looking east through my office window into the beautiful blue skies of a mild winter day. Though the view is lovely, my heart is saddened.

Thirty-five years ago today, my wife and I were sitting at our table enjoying an early lunch when a friend called to tell us the launch of the Challenger space shuttle had just occurred. It was a cool, beautiful, and clear day in central Florida and this launch was a historical one. Among the passengers on the shuttle was thirty-seven-year-old Christa McAuliffe, a high school teacher from New Hampshire and the first civilian to go into space. This launch was a fascinating one as a result, and the world was watching. We had had the privilege of visiting NASA facilities and, from our vantage point only sixty miles from Cape Canaveral, had seen quite clearly various launches in the past. However, today was different.

It was on that chilly, beautiful, clear day, January 28, 1986, we ran outside to view the spectacle, only to soon cringe in disbelief and horror as the Space Shuttle Challenger exploded in plain sight. Every time I see pictures replayed of this event, my mind goes back to that paralyzing moment when we watched as trails of smoke and metal debris filled the sky as one of America's greatest tragedies unfolded.

Elizabeth Chuck, in an article for NBC News, reflects on the event through the eyes of Bob Eberling, one of the engineers on the Challenger project:

> It was a chilly January morning and Bob Ebeling, an employee at NASA contractor Morton Thiokol, was panicking. As a booster rocket engineer, Ebeling had intimate knowledge of how the space shuttle Challenger would perform in cold weather. And the rubber O-ring seals designed to keep burning rocket fuel from leaking from the Challenger's booster joints hadn't been tested in temperatures this low. "They had tested the O-ring to something like 38 degrees, and it was only 28 degrees when they launched," Ebeling's daughter, Leslie Serna, 63, told NBC News on Thursday. "He said, 'It's going to be a catastrophic event ... The Challenger's going to blow up." After looking at the forecast the night before, Ebeling and four fellow engineers begged for the launch to be postponed until it warmed up. But their managers, and NASA, refused. So, on January 28, 1986, Ebeling sat in a conference room surrounded by Morton Thiokol executives, powerless, and watched the Challenger take off on a big-screen TV. About 75 seconds after liftoff, it exploded, killing its crew of seven. And for years, he could not forgive himself.[6]

The amazing thing about this account and others related to the Challenger disaster is that it appears the incident was avoidable.

Perhaps a little more accountability from political and other partnering entities could have prevented the explosion? That may never be known, but what we know is that this explosion resulted from a relatively very small thing. According to the records from the Report of the Presidential Commission on the Space Shuttle Challenger Accident, the "loss of the Space Shuttle Challenger was caused by a failure in the joint between the two lower segments of the right Solid Rocket Motor. The specific failure was the destruction of the seals intended to prevent hot gases from leaking through the joint during the propellant burn of the rocket motor."[7] Almost unbelievable is the fact that the two O-rings that failed to seal the leaky joint measured only .28 of an inch in diameter![8]

Small things can make a huge difference!

When Small Stuff Becomes a Big Deal

King Asa is a prime example of how a leader can be very effective for decades, but then in later years after great success, a character flaw is revealed that causes the leader's impact to diminish. For Asa, the weakness seems to have been fear that caused the king to pursue a confederacy with an enemy. The ungodly alliance with Syria displeased God and resulted in upheaval in the nation of Judah for the rest of Asa's reign.

Throughout the ages, leaders have succumbed to various personal flaws that have also caused great personal and professional difficulties.

It is quite astounding how many leaders fall prey to the tendency to self-destruct after years of a very successful career. In his very insightful book, *The Paradox of Success*,[9] John O'Neil describes how all leaders must beware of a "shadow side" that often accompanies virtues that otherwise lend toward success. For example, one's strong work ethic might morph into a very unhealthy workaholic tendency if ignoring honest and consistent self-evaluation.

Though writing several years ago, O'Neil has provided a masterful view of the prevalence, variety, and destructive nature of shadow tendencies and how these tend to hide very stealthily behind the blazing flames of success and leadership effectiveness. Nothing could be more relevant to the 21st-century leader bombarded with "legitimate" demands and expectations to perform. These pressures seem to leave little time or energy for self-reflection and evaluation. In this results-oriented climate, the "shadow side" can thrive and eventually emerge with a vengeance. Great intentionality is required to stave off this ever-present danger.

One reason a person overlooks the shadow side is that, in the overall scheme of things, these negative tendencies can appear to be "small stuff." Small blemishes, however, can be very costly. A 2015 article published by the Huffington Post explains the concept of cosmetic filtering: "An estimated six billion pounds of fruits and vegetables are wasted every year in the US, with some of those fruits and vegetables wasted because they are ugly, according to a report by the Natural Resources Defense Council. This means a portion of the produce grown for human consumption is rejected by grocery stores and goes uneaten because of its appearance."[10] While a revision in 2017 to the original article changed the amount of waste stated, the fact remains that ignoring what might seem like a "small" issue can result in huge losses! How sad this story is for the food industry and the starving around the world.

How much sadder when leaders from all organizational contexts let "blemishes" caused by ignoring a "shadow side" negatively impact their personal lives and the lives of those they are leading! The "small stuff" that becomes a big deal comes in many varieties.

Small Stuff? – Excessive Self-confidence

There is no doubt that confidence is a crucial trait in leadership. The apostle Paul sheds light on the issue of "sufficiency" for the task when writing, "Not that we are sufficient of ourselves to think of anything as being from ourselves, but our sufficiency is from God" (2 Cor. 3:5). Apparent here is that God wants those leading to have a confidence that comes from understanding His provision that is enough for the job at hand. It is also evident in the passage that a leader's perspective, competence, and corresponding confidence is not to come from an exaggerated sense of personal ability and overinflated ego!

Unfortunately, it appears there is often only a small step from God-confidence to self-confidence. As the Lord has granted a prosperous outcome for endeavors undertaken, the temptation arises to look in the mirror to place the accompanying accolades. Thus, the downhill spiral into glory-hogging and self-sufficiency begins. Indicators begin to appear of this subtle shift, and signs that are obvious to others but often invisible to the leaders afflicted.

When giving credit, language changes from uses of "we" and "they" where praise of deflected to the ever-increasing use of first-person "I," where recognition is both received and expected! One's personal devotional time is neglected due to the increased feelings of importance and "need" demanding more and more time and energy. Busyness serves well to ego-stroke and confirms one's certainty of a competence and presence that all are desperate for. The leader who goes down this path and remains too long will soon find themselves wallowing in the quagmire of frustration, depression, burnout, cynicism, and isolation.

Of course, the remedy for this is to maintain a proper assessment of oneself in the light of God's gifts and personal weaknesses. Confidence derived from this balanced perspective is healthy, liberating, and empowering to others!

Some of the best advice one can receive is something that was shared with me years ago by a friend named Frank Williams. Frank was much older and a very successful salesman in a major industrial chemical company. One day, I shared with him how every time I got in front of a group to speak, I was almost sick because of the emotions and pressure of the moment. I described this as "many butterflies in my stomach." Frank surprised me in responding with two words of wisdom: 1) "If you ever get rid of the butterflies, you will be in trouble." This indicates too much self-confidence; 2) "The secret is not getting rid of the butterflies but making them fly in formation!"

Here's the balance between being too confident in one's own abilities and finding confidence that comes when being prepared but ultimately dependent on God's touch!

Small Stuff? – Arrogant Listening

Leaders who have experienced a significant amount of success in their organizational context must be careful not to succumb to the practice of what might be called "arrogant listening." This problem happens when an individual either refuses to genuinely listen to others or is overly selective about those allowed to speak into a situation or decision. While acknowledging the obvious need to limit the amount of "cooks in the kitchen," it should also be recognized that leaders can slip into a mode where they leave some who should have a voice on the outside-looking-in.

Sometimes this problem occurs when opinions expressed are perceived by the leader to be overly negative and thus non-confirming. Such was indeed the case with King Asa as he was rebuked by Hanani, the seer, for pursuing an alliance with the king of Syria rather than putting his trust in Yahweh (2 Chron. 16:6-10). Asa succumbed to the pressures of the nation's immediate threat, which yielded a word of judgment from the Lord through the prophet. Rather than humbly submit to the instructions of Yahweh, the arrogant king treated Hanani with hatred and imprisonment while also proceeding to be abusive to others around him. Rejection of God's direction brought difficulty to the nation for quite a time to come and caused Asa suffering until his death. What problems arise when a leader becomes so arrogant in their own opinion that they refuse to give heed to those that God may send as a messenger on a rescue mission![11]

Arrogant listening can also occur when a leader develops a preconceived tunnel-vision of what must qualify someone who will be allowed to have a voice. Arrogance in leadership tends to raise the bar extremely high in this regard. As a result, the leader may miss the very insight God would send because it is coming through a seemingly "unqualified" vessel. Leaders must be careful to be sensitive to those around them in that God often chooses to use "the weak things of this world to confound the mighty" (1 Cor. 1:27b). May we never disregard a "David" because he does not have the outward appearance of a king (1 Sam. 16:7b). May we never overlook a little boy's lunch as "so little among so many" (John. 6:9). It could be that God will take the shepherd boy and make him the most renowned king in Israel's history. It could be that God will take the picnic lunch of a child and use it to perform the only miracle (besides the resurrection) recorded in all four gospel accounts.

It could be that your valuable wisdom to a leadership dilemma at hand may be on the lips of someone outside the "normal" leadership circle. Are you listening?

Small Stuff? – Accelerated Entitlement

Entitlement has been the topic of much conversation and research in recent years, especially as it relates to perceived characteristics of the Millennial generation. This consideration is vital in that this age group presently comprises a significant part of the workforce. However, it is interesting to note that much entitlement tends to creep into the offices of the well-established, not just the new-kids-on-the-block. The entitlement trap is a deep and dangerous abyss awaiting successful leaders. When a leader finds themselves expecting ever-increasing perks, benefits, accolades, etc. because of a job well done, red flags fly high in that the monster of "I deserve this" (entitlement in a nutshell) is looming hungrily on the horizon.

Most assuredly, successful leaders should be compensated well and appreciated much for their expertise, efforts, and energies that help lead to corporate wins. Serious problems are lurking, nonetheless, when these things become primary expectations driven by a "my rights" stance rather than an appreciation founded on a "joy of service" mentality.

One of the most powerful and well-known leadership statements from recent years is from former Fortune 500 CEO, Max De Pree. In his book, *Leadership Is An Art*, De Pree states, "The first responsibility of a leader is to define reality. The last is to say thank you. In between the two, the leader must become a servant and a debtor. That sums up the progress of an artful leader."[12] Understanding and implementing the leadership style proposed by this highly successful executive creates a leadership culture characterized by vision, yes, but also by servanthood and a strong sense of gratitude.

In this paradigm, the all-too-common bent toward entitlement gives way to a much greater productivity climate with longer-term results. Members of the team begin to feel a strong foundation of support and camaraderie and a genuine appreciation exuding from the leader around them. Leaders are not only increasingly thankful for the team members and the work accomplished but also maintain a real sense of gratitude for the opportunity and position of influence they have. As leaders consistently express a hardy "thank you," everybody wins!

At this moment, perhaps it would be a good time to pause and do some introspection as to where leadership position and success has taken us? Are we ever contemplating how "I deserve more for all that I do?" or do we remain continually grateful for the privilege of serving others in a manner that assists them in being prosperous and fulfilled. Is gratitude for where we are and for with whom we have the opportunity to interact an ever-increasing focus and goal?

These, my friend, are critical questions for any leader in a day where "I'm gonna get mine" is the prevailing mantra!

Small Stuff? – Weak Fences

I will never forget the first time we visited the Grand Canyon. "That big hole in the ground" was indeed impressive, and the colors that danced on the canyon walls as the sun was setting were absolutely mesmerizing. The most amazing thing to me on that first sighting, however, was there were no fences! People can actually walk right up to the edge with no protective barriers and, if getting too close, fall to a horrible and tragic death. This lack of barriers was scary.

My heart breaks as I write this final section for this chapter, and I am literally fighting back the tears. My wife just came in and asked, "Did you hear about _____," a very well- known international teacher/evangelist accused of multiple layers of sexual misconduct. Being familiar with the investigations related to this going on for over a year, my immediate response was, "Don't tell me it's true!" Unfortunately, it appears that this powerful speaker and apologist was, in reality, living a double life. It is also apparent that much of the problem resulted from constant travels without proper personal accountability structures in place. Having no or very weak fences is a bad idea!

Several years ago, the liberal media lampooned former United States vice-president Mike Pence for a "fence" he maintained for personal and professional protection.[13] The practice of not being in any situation of potential compromise with the opposite sex was related to one of four practices of Billy Graham's Modesto Manifesto[14]. "We will be exemplary in morals—clear, clean, and careful to avoid the very appearance of impropriety." Dr. Graham's team agreed early on to practice extreme caution in this area of vulnerability, and Mr. Pence took his lead from this very powerful and successful evangelist's example.

Other areas of the Manifesto dealt with not only sexual immorality but with the "shady handling of money…Badmouthing others doing similar work… (and) exaggerating accomplishments."[15] Most people would agree these areas present very perilous potential pitfalls to any leader in any context. The problem results when success so magnifies a leader's persona that the leader begins to feel invincible and thus vastly underestimates a danger at hand. Myra and Shelley warn, "It's easy to wink at the word temptation, to flirt with extramarital sex, or to shade the truth just a little, or to arrange corporate finances for just a little personal benefit. It's easy to believe that the consequences of playing a little loose with temptations will be minor."[16]

A big deal becomes a small issue, and a deadly land mine becomes a firecracker. So sure of their ability to maintain proper footing regardless, these leaders ignore the warning signs and fences (if there is one!) and wander way too close to the edge. When the drop off is one-mile deep, and sudden death is the inevitable result, only the foolish will see how close they can get to the edge without falling!

That final and fatal step will never be worth it.

Diligence in Success

Note the title to these closing words: Diligence IN Success. All understand the work it takes to be diligent FOR success; few often take the time to stop and think what it takes to stay diligent IN a place of success and favor. Accomplishing notable things with many blessed as a result is a great thing, as long as it does become the demise of the successful one as they blow themselves up through neglect of the little things that tend to creep in around them. We could have talked about several other "small stuff" concerns in this chapter (excessive fear of failure, neglect of physical and mental health, etc.). Still, the issues discussed should suffice to alert one again of the dangers that accompany success and influence.

John McKee, in an excellent blog response, reminds readers of the battle all leaders must war for ongoing self-reflection and personal growth, increasing professional competence, and interpersonal sensitivity and effectiveness. McKee declares, "the executive suite is not so sweet."[17] For sure, the journey is never comfortable, though always worth the fight.

Leadership is a wonderful calling with a marvelous opportunity to make a difference in the lives of many. No wonder the struggles to the place of much fruit are great. No wonder the relentless fight to lead well for the duration, not just a season, is something that never ends!

Enjoy the magnificent views that surround you on the journey, my leader friend! Just don't get too close to the edge… it's a long way down.

Chapter Three – King Jehoshaphat (873-848) 1 Kings 22; 2 Kings 3; 2 Chronicles 17-20

King Jehoshaphat proved to be a bright spot in the Judean narrative. Like his father, Asa, the biblical text gives him high marks in many areas, particularly in his religious faith, his military victories, and his sensitivity to the prophetic voice. His main weakness lay with his nature of being too trusting of others. In this respect, he proved to be naïve at times with long-lasting negative effects. The four major descriptions of his reign are worth exploring.

1. He was a Good King

Jehoshaphat's mother was Azubah. The only other woman in the Bible with this name was Caleb's wife, who had lived more than five centuries earlier. If Azubah's parents named her with the connection to the famous Caleb, we may have an indication of Jehoshaphat's mentoring example. The venerated Caleb had a diligent and consistent nature that inspired many future generations to name their sons after him. By making Caleb's wife the namesake for their daughter, Azubah's parents indicated the character qualities they desired in her (and her future offspring). Most likely, Azubah made a positive impact on her son.

During his reign, Jehoshaphat attempted numerous reforms. It is fitting that his name means "Yahweh has judged." He reorganized the judicial system to ensure justice throughout his land. He installed ethical judges and distributed them throughout the land to ensure consistent rulings. In like fashion, he sent teachers throughout Judah with a strong educational training. Finally, he tore down the Canaanite high places. The people incorrectly continued to sacrifice to Yahweh at places of their own choosing, rather than the commanded centralized location; however, Jehoshaphat exemplified major efforts in eliminating Canaanite idolatry.

A succinct summary of Jehoshaphat is "He trusted God and sought him." He never wavered from this consistent pattern. His kingdom became firmly established. Favor abounded to him. Great riches and honor came to him. Thankfully, we read that the riches and honor did not corrupt him. Indeed, he was an exceptionally good king.

2. He was a Naïve King

As previously noted, the king had a major weakness in his trusting nature toward others. People who have a good core quite easily assume others also have a good core. The reality is that not everyone can, or should, be trusted. We see numerous examples of Jehoshaphat's excessive trusting soul.

First, he allied himself through marriage with King Ahab and Queen Jezebel of Israel. (Ahab is found in Assyrian and Moabite inscriptions.)[18] Ahab and Jezebel's daughter, Athaliah, and Jehoshaphat's son, Jehoram, would marry. Previously, Ahab's father Omri and Jezebel's father Ethbaal had created their arranged marriage to solidify peace between Phoenicia and Israel. The ill-fated union brought Baalism into the northern tribes with disastrous results. As we will see in the next chapter, Jehoshaphat's and Ahab's similarly arranged marriage with their children tragically carried Baalism into the southern kingdom of Judah. This foolish decision came close to destroying the Davidic line.

Second, after his dreadful decision to have his son marry Ahab's daughter, he also agreed to align himself militarily with Ahab. Jehoshaphat unwisely joined himself and his army with King Ahab in an ill-fated battle with Syria. After Ahab's strong urging, Jehoshaphat replied, "I am as you are, and my people as your people; we will join you in the war."

To compound this foolish offer, Ahab suggested, "I will enter the battle in disguise, but you will wear your royal robes." In other words, "While I hide, you become the main target of the enemy's offense." Unbelievably, Jehoshaphat gullibly agreed. The Syrian forces turned on the leader in regal clothing (Jehoshaphat) and he almost lost his life. In spite of the disguise, a Syrian archer shot at random and mortally struck the disguised Ahab. The northern king died, and the southern king returned home in defeat.

Third, he made an agreement with the wicked King Amaziah, the son of Ahab. Jehoshaphat and Amaziah jointly decided to build ships in the port area of the Red Sea. However, a storm arose and destroyed their ships. Comparing the two reports from Kings and Chronicles, it appears that Amaziah might have desired to continue with the undertaking, but Jehoshaphat called off any further endeavors with Amaziah and the project.

3. He was a Military King

The narrative spends a good deal of space describing and complimenting Jehoshaphat's military preparations. He put garrisons in northern cities that his father Asa had captured. He stationed troops in all the fortified cities of Judah. He built additional forts and store cities in Judah. He had large supplies in the towns of Judah. He placed experienced fighting men in the capital city of Jerusalem. The Philistines brought gifts to him. Similarly, the Arabs brought gifts.

A significant point is made that the fear of the Lord fell on all the kingdoms of the lands surrounding Judah, so that they did not go to war with Jehoshaphat for a good portion of his reign. In the latter part of his reign, a vast combined army from Ammon, Moab, and Edom came up against the Judean nation. The invasion entered from Judah's southeastern region.

The king stationed musicians and singers ahead of his army as they approached the invaders. When the music and singing arose, confusion within the enemy's camp also arose. In the confusion, the enemy troops turned on each other. The devastation that the enemy troops inflicted on each other eliminated the need for Judah to even fight. The remainder of the enemy fled the battle, leaving behind a great deal of plunder, clothing, and weapons. Again, the text repeats an earlier comment, "The fear of the Lord came upon the surrounding nations." However, an additional comment adds, "The king had peace the rest of his reign."

4. He was a Prophetic King

By listing him as a prophetic king, we are revealing the significant value that King Jehoshaphat placed on the prophetic voice in his day. He was known as a king who personally sought the Lord. He also commended the prophetic ministry to his people. He accepted encouragement, direction, and even correction from the prophets. We find five occasions where the prophetic voice intersected with his reign.

First, before Jehoshaphat and Ahab went to battle against Syria, the prophets were consulted. Four hundred prophets, who were already aligned with Ahab, prophesied total success in battle. Jehoshaphat must have had a check in his own spirit, for he requested yet another prophet be consulted. The prophet Micaiah (not to be confused with the southern prophet Micah) predicted defeat of the combined Jewish armies by the Syrians. Additionally, he predicted the death of King Ahab in battle. Both of these predictions were fulfilled.

Second, after Jehoshaphat returned home safely from battle, he was met by the prophet Jehu, son of the prophet Hanani. In previous years, Jehu had prophesied the demise of the northern king Baasha, which was fulfilled. Jehu's father, Hanani, had also prophesied to King Asa of Judah, the father of Jehoshaphat. King Asa did not like Hanani's correction and put him in prison. Jehoshaphat knew this history and the accuracy of this prophetic family.

Jehu's words both corrected and complimented King Jehoshaphat. As to the correction, Jehoshaphat had aligned himself with Ahab who was an enemy of the Lord. Jehu warned the king that serious consequences were possible. As to the compliment, Jehu accented Jehoshaphat's efforts at reform and his heart at seeking the Lord. The effect seemed positive upon the king, for he implemented even greater reforms in Judah.

Third, Jahaziel prophesied to King Jehoshaphat and his army when they faced the combined forces of three nations. He encouraged the troops in the midst of battle. He informed the troops where the enemy was located, which proved to be correct. Finally, Jahaziel made the amazing prediction that Judah would not even need to fight, which also was fulfilled. Jahaziel began and ended with a message to "fear not."

Fourth, Eliezer prophesied to King Jehoshaphat about his alignment with Ahab's wicked successor, Ahaziah. The two kings conceived a plan to build ships in Judah's southern port on the Red Sea. The prophetic portrait was sharp and to the point, "Because of this alliance with Ahaziah, your ships will be destroyed." Indeed, the ships were destroyed, and Jehoshaphat did not continue with the project.

Fifth, Elisha prophesied to both King Jehoram (Ahab's son), and to King Jehoshaphat. In 2013, archaeologists found a unique house that may be a prophet's home dating to Elisha's time and location.[19] The ostracon within the house had the name of Elisha on them. The two Jewish kings had combined their armies to fight against the nation of Moab. This Moabite rebellion may be referenced on a Moabite altar, recently found in 2010.[20]

Elisha had no respect for Jehoram and stated so; however, he was complimentary toward Jehoshaphat. Elisha prophesied the success of their battle against Moab. The prophecy was fulfilled; however, the Moabite king, Mesha, sacrificed his son on the walls of the city. His famous stele speaks of his rebellion from Jewish rule.[21] The horrific act disgusted the Jewish army and they returned home. Egyptian records report similar Canaanite child sacrifices during intense battles.[22]

Conclusion on King Jehoshaphat

The overall narrative of Jehoshaphat remains positive. He had a tender heart toward the things of God. He diligently and faithfully sought to eliminate idolatry throughout the land. He wisely prepared the nation militarily. He bravely led in battle, reformed the judicial system, and instituted a nationwide education program. He valued the prophets even when they scolded him. Yet, he was overly trusting on occasion, and we will see in the next chapter the fruit of those naïve arrangements.

Application - Chapter 3 – Jehoshaphat - "A Desperate Confidence"

As I sat in these meetings, I was amazed.

The two leadership-related meetings were very different, several years apart, and served very different purposes. However, the impact made by the two executive leaders involved was so lasting and positive that those moments of interaction still linger in my mind. One meeting related to a new paradigm of operation needing discussion, review, and implementation, while the other was a quasi-interview of a potential new senior leader for the organization. As I sat in both contexts, my ears were wide open to issues on the table as we all recognized the potential impact of those conversations' outcomes.

Sometime in the process, though for very different reasons, both leaders made a similar comment that "sealed the deal" from my perspective. While I do not remember the exact wordings, the overall gist and climate is clear. In the strategic planning meeting, the executive leader said, "Here's the deal. I don't know what to do and which direction we need to take at this moment. But I promise you this; we will figure this out and together make it happen!" In meeting two, the interview for a senior position, the candidate stopped in the middle of the questioning and said to all sitting around, "I know I will be getting in over my head… However, I can tell you now that I will do what needs to be done, with the help of God, to figure this out and do it with excellence!"

What was obvious from both of these very talented and accomplished leaders was the humility to recognize and admit a "cluelessness" that was somewhat liberating and admirable. This glimpse of vulnerability was very endearing, allowing those present to, in my view, let down defenses and grant a certain level of credibility and corresponding trust. Along with honesty and transparency, there also exuded a strength of confidence that included a need for God's intervention and team participation. When we left both of those meetings, I knew that the tandem characteristics of "desperate confidence" had won the day and solidified the leadership of those involved.

While the phrase "desperate confidence" may appear to some to be an oxymoron, it is indeed the key to leading effectively in turbulent times.

Permanent White-water

While penning this chapter, the United States and the entire world are in the throes of a crisis as no one in this generation has ever experienced or could have imagined. Havoc among every societal system on planet earth and changes to personal and institutional lives forever changed by the COVID 19 pandemic.

Leaders from every sector are scrambling to determine the "next step" as media outlets inundate hearts and minds with a tidal wave of information that is often quite confusing and conflicting. Whether one is listening to the President from a White House briefing, a local school superintendent, business gurus relating trends from Wall Street, or pastors of local churches, similar things are being heard. We have not been here before, we are not sure what is next, but we will try to figure this out. Whatever context you consider, everyday life situations' relatively predictable flow has drastically (and overnight!) given way to very turbulent and unpredictable currents that demand attention.

Some years ago, organizational behavior and change specialist Dr. Peter Vaill wrote two books that, whether he recognized it or not, proved to be quite prophetic as related to societal transitions. In his books, *Managing as a Performing Art*[23] and later, *Learning as a State of Being,*[24] Vaill explains that successfully navigating future trends, opportunities, and challenges in any organizational (or personal) context will require both a mindset and skills akin to riding the waves of whitewater rafting. The days of relaxingly rowing the peaceful trickles of a sunlit, tranquil lake have given way to a much more turbulent challenge. This challenge of whitewater, per Vaill, includes several characteristics that indicate the whitewater season is upon us: 1) Conditions full of surprises, 2) Complex systems producing novel problems, 3) Events that are "messy" and ill-structured, 4) Events that are often extremely costly, 5) Problems of recurrence. As one examines this list and compares it with the intense dilemmas leaders are facing at this moment, there can be little doubt that whitewater, and the uncertainties it brings, is upon us.

The good news in all of this is that there is a leadership style especially effective in whitewater seasons: the desperate but confident leader! King Jehoshaphat is an example of a leader from times past that faced very difficult and dangerous times but, through desperate confidence, succeeded in thriving amid the threats on the horizon.

Jehoshaphat's Plea

A very revelatory incident in Judah's life and their King Jehoshaphat is recorded in 2 Chronicles 20. This passage opens with the record of three powerful armies approaching to challenge a very vulnerable and militarily inferior Judean kingdom. Upon learning of the impending and potentially devastating attack looming on the horizon, Jehoshaphat gives orders to gather "all of Judah" together to pray and seek the Lord (vss. 1-4).

It is interesting to note that the king does not require this only of others but leads the intercessory convocation with his presence and petition (vss. 5-13). Leading in uncertain times requires leaders to be a part of the people, not apart from the people! In his petition, Jehoshaphat brings to remembrance God's promises to protect His inheritance (His people) and to hear them when they cry out in seasons of intense threats from surrounding forces. Additionally, the king prefaces all by affirming the understanding that God is the actual owner of all, and the nation was simply a steward of the gracious and generous allowances received as His people.

The final plea of Jehoshaphat's petition reveals the heart of this king, his posture of humility, and his ultimate sense of hope: "Oh, our God, will You not judge them? For we have no power against this great multitude that is coming against us; nor do we know what to do, but our eyes are upon You" (vs. 12, NKJV). Three phrases reveal implications and applications that should be constant and encouraging reminders that 21st leaders should take to heart: 1) It is okay to feel POWERLESS ("we have no power against this"); 2) It is okay to feel CLUELESS ("nor do we know what to do"); and 3) It is empowering to be RELY on Him!

Our times stretch human ingenuity and copycat tendencies to the breaking point and are causing leaders to realize the impotence of previously successful strategies and assumptions. However, rather than wringing our hands in despair, God is graciously inviting us through the present dilemmas to find in Him our source of strength, stability, and success once again. He is granting us a desperate confidence!

Jehoshaphat's Plan

Following the humble and sincere petition, the king and the people stand waiting in the presence of God for an answer (vs. 13). True confidence results from knowing that intercession can result in both an internal sense of calm that prevents one from reacting in panic (almost always destructive and counter-productive) and a workable plan for execution. God is not just interested in soothing our fears in

His presence but providing direction and strength for implementation by His Spirit!

The plan revealed to the king was, once again, an opportunity to exercise a desperate confidence. This battle was going to be won by the singers rather than by the soldiers! Shouts of praise and songs of deliverance are to be on the Levites' lips and worship leaders as God instructs them to lead the people toward the encroaching enemies (vss. 14-19). This worship serves to further acknowledge God's preeminence in the preservation of His people. While surely seeming strange as related to conventional warfare methods, God's plan worked (it always will!). God's plan ushered in God's presence, and God's presence prevailed as He set the enemy forces in disarray without one arrow shot from the bow of a Judean warrior (vss. 20-24)!

Could it be that there is a direct connection between the miraculous intervention so needed in 21st-century contexts and a leader's desperate confidence?

Jehoshaphat's Provision

When all the dust had settled from the confrontation and divinely instigated confusion, Judah and King Jehoshaphat must have been shocked to find that God had not only routed the enemy but had also provided incredible booty for the taking (vss. 25-28)! Just protection from the devastation would surely have been deliverance enough, but God will often not stop with "enough." A desperate confidence will bring forth, at times, results that far surpass anything we could have ever imagined (Eph. 3:20)!

The end of this story notes that wealth and physical provision are not the only spoils from this victory. The fact that "the fear of God" and Jehoshaphat's influence spread over the surrounding areas (vss. 29-30) is no simple sidenote to the narrative. When a leader is willing to operate out of a "desperate confidence," greater opportunity to give God glory results. Rather than bringing into question one's leadership competency, a desperate confidence will tend to yield a catapulting of a leader's credibility (more on that later) to new levels in the perspective of organizational constituents.

Leaders should be encouraged to know people are not expecting an invincible, have-all-the-answers-all-the-time superhero to lead them!

Desperate confidence is far from being an oil versus water mixture. This leadership characteristic creates a climate that glorifies God, where people find fulfillment in engagement, and where followers deem leadership credible and worthy of respect. It sounds like a win-win-win to me!

Chapter Four – Jehoram, Ahaziah, and Athaliah (853-835) 2 Kings 8-11; 2 Chronicles 21-24

The concluding paragraph on King Jehoshaphat lists the names of his seven sons. The short statement that Jehoram was chosen because he was the firstborn implies that the only reason Jehoram was chosen was his birth order. The stage is now set for this chapter covering the reigns of Jehoshaphat's son, daughter-in-law, and grandson. Due to the unique nature of these three Judean leaders, we will view them as a cohesive whole.

In 1993, a tablet was discovered at the archaeological site of Tel Dan.[25] The names on the famous plaque are the same people in our present chapter, and the tablet dates back to the same biblical period we are reviewing. Key players on the tablet are Jehoram, son of Ahab, and Ahaziah, son of Jehoram, of the house of David. The two theories of authorship proposed are either Hazael of Syria or Jehu of Israel. Inscriptions from Hazael have been found.[26] Additionally, Jehu is pictured on the Black Obelisk, discovered in 1846, paying tribute to the Assyrian king, Shalmaneser III.[27]

1. King Jehoram

After Jehoram was established as king, he viciously murdered all his brothers and some of the officials of Judah. At this time, murder entered into the Judean royal family. The root influence of these acts of murder are linked to Jehoram's marriage to the wicked Athaliah. She was the daughter of King Ahab and Queen Jezebel of Israel. Her parents did murderous acts that she would have seen from childhood. During this period, both kings of Judah and Israel had the same name of Jehoram (Joram). They were brothers-in-law due to the marriage with Athaliah.

The narrative criticizes the Judean king Jehoram for walking in the same ways as his father-in-law Ahab. As such, Jehoram built high places to the Canaanite gods, caused the people to prostrate themselves, and led Judah astray. The same evil Baal worship that contaminated the northern kingdom had spread southward into Judah. The archaeologists have found much in the way of evidence of child sacrifice associated with the practice of Baalism.[28] King Jehoram committed serious atrocities, and he reaped serious repercussions.

First, the eastern kingdom of Edom rebelled against Judah. King Jehoram went to battle against the Edomites seeking to quell the uprising. He not only lost the battle, but almost lost his life. Edom remained independent of Judah's oversight for years. Most importantly, Judea lost control of all the lucrative, eastern trade routes.

Second, the western Judean city of Libnah also rebelled against Jehoram. Libnah was a Levitical town that Joshua had designated as a city of refuge. The Jewish inhabitants of Libnah may have become so incensed at Jehoram's flagrant idol worship that they succeeded from the Judean nation.

Third, the prophet Elijah wrote a foreboding letter to Jehoram. Elijah is only mentioned once in 2 Chronicles and it is in regard to this letter. He may have written his letter prior to his departure and left instructions for its delivery. The prophet chided the king for not following in the steps of his father, King Jehoshaphat, but following in the ways of his father-in-law, King Ahab. The prophet predicted that Jehoram would die a gruesome death in which his bowels would painfully come out. Indeed, Jehoram endured his last two years with an incurable disease of the bowels in which they came out. When he died after an eight-year reign, the people did not regret his death. He was not buried in the royal tombs.

Fourth, Elijah's letter further confronted Jehoram's murder of his own brothers, whom the prophet described as "being better than you." The prophet foretold the destruction that would soon fall on Jehoram and his family. This word, too, was fulfilled when a coalition of Arabs, Ethiopians, and Philistines attacked Judah. They carried off the treasure in the king's palace. Additionally, the coalition took captive all of Jehoram's sons and their wives, with the exception of one of his sons. As Jehoram had killed six of his father's seven sons, so now he lost all but one son. That one son was Ahaziah, the youngest.

2. King Ahaziah (Jehoahaz)

King Ahaziah ruled only one year, and he began his short reign at age twenty-two. Like his father Jehoram, he followed in the evil ways of King Ahab, due to the negative influence of Athaliah, the daughter of Ahab and Jezebel. Also, the northern kingdom's advisors became Ahaziah's advisors. The northern king Jehoram was Ahaziah's uncle. Nothing good came out of Jehoram's misguided mentoring of Ahaziah.

Prior to this timeframe, the prophet Elisha prophesied to the Syrian military commander Hazael. The message proclaimed that Hazael would one day become king of Syria. Indeed, Hazael did become the king; however, he took matters into his own hands and assassinated his predecessor. Additionally, Elisha anointed Jehu via a student prophet. Jehu commanded the northern Israel army. The prophetic message stated that he would one day "become king of Israel. He would eliminate the house of Ahab and Jezebel for their murders of prophets and other innocent people. He would eradicate Baalism out of Israel."

Eventually the Jewish nations of Israel and Judah formed a coalition against King Hazael, the new usurper of Syria. King Jehoram of Israel and his nephew King Ahaziah of Judah fought against Hazael and his forces. In the battle, King Jehoram was seriously wounded. Due to the grave nature of his wounds, Jehoram was forced to return to his own land to recover from his battle injuries.

Later, King Ahaziah decided to visit his uncle, King Jehoram. The purpose of the visit was to see how his uncle was healing from his wounds. Perhaps due to King Jehoram's injuries, Jehu chose this opportune moment to rebel against his king. Jehu managed not only to kill King Jehoram of Israel, but also his visiting nephew, King

Ahaziah of Judah.

The record in 2 Chronicles gives the broader Samaritan region for Ahaziah's death. The word Samaria is used as often for the region of Israel as the capital city. The point of 2 Chronicles is that the southern king died in the northern region while wrongly aligned with his idolatrous relatives.

The record of 2 Kings gives the more specific location and details of Ahaziah's death in the north. 2 Kings tends to provide more details on the northern kingdom; however, 2 Chronicles focuses more on the southern kingdom of Judah.

Only out of respect for the late King Jehoshaphat, the grandfather of Ahaziah, King Jehu had Ahaziah properly buried. Jehu traveled to Queen Jezebel's location and ensured that the evil woman died. Jehu also killed Ahab's other sons. The prophecies of the ultimate destruction of Ahab's and Jezebel's household were almost complete. Only one more remained — their wicked daughter, Athaliah.

3. Queen Athaliah

Upon the death of King Ahaziah, his mother Athaliah seized the throne of Judah. In her first orders as queen, she proceeded to destroy the entire royal family of Judah. She killed any legitimate rival. She even killed her own offspring, including her grandchildren. The Davidic dynasty almost ceased in the first days of her evil six-year reign. Only one of Athaliah's grandsons, Jehoash (Joash), survived.

In the chaotic slaughter of innocent children, a hero arose. A woman named Jehosheba and an unnamed nurse, bravely saved the one-year-old's life. Jehosheba removed little Jehoash from the massacre undetected. She then hid the child with the nurse in a bedroom. The queen's henchmen must have reported all were dead. The butcher queen wrongly assumed that all threats to her position were gone.

Jehosheba was the aunt of young Jehoash. Her brother was the late King Ahaziah of Judah. She was a daughter of King Jehoram, but not necessarily of Athaliah. Additionally, Jehosheba was the wife of the godly high priest, Jehoiada. For six years, Jehosheba and Jehoiada courageously managed to hide Jehoash. Of all places, they hid him in the Jewish temple. The decision proved to be a wise one. Queen Athaliah worshipped at the temple of Baal. Most likely she rarely, if ever, visited the Jewish temple.

After six years passed, Jehoiada and the priests made their move. The now seven-year-old Joash was publicly crowned king, accompanied with great music and celebration. The loud coronation drew Queen Athaliah to the temple where she saw the young king in regal attire. Her wicked reign came to an end that day. Upon her execution the people of Judah rejoiced, and the city of Jerusalem was calm.

Conclusion on King Jehoram, King Ahaziah, and Queen Athaliah

The domino effect of Ahab's arranged marriage to the Phoenician Jezebel tumbled downward. Their daughter, Athaliah, married Jehoshaphat's son, Jehoram. Downward still, six of Jehoshaphat's seven sons were murdered by their own brother, Jehoram. The dominoes continued to topple. Jehoram would lose all his sons except his youngest, Ahaziah. After a short reign of only one year, Ahaziah was executed by Jehu's men. Also, 42 of Ahaziah's relatives were executed by Jehu. The downward domino effect continued. Ahaziah's wicked mother, Athaliah, came within a hair's breadth of exterminating the entire Davidic line. These alliances proved deadly.

In spite of this murderous drama, hope shone through. The godly leadership of Judah tore down the temple of Baal and executed the priest of Baal. Jehoram, Ahaziah, and Athaliah met untimely deaths. The dynasty of the wicked rulers Ahab and Jezebel came to an end in both Israel and Judah. Both Jewish kingdoms took major steps to eradicate the evil imported by Baalism from Phoenicia.

Application - Chapter 4 - Jehoram, Ahaziah, and Athaliah - The Enemy In You

As is obvious from some of the book's previous chapters, I have made my share of mistakes while on the leadership journey. However, occasionally, I got it right. The following account is one of those times!

While pastoring, I was blessed to have a great staff giving oversight to several key areas of the church's ministry. Among those was a young man whose job description focused primarily on youth ministry but whose gift mix included a very powerful ability to preach with strong passion and significant substance. The congregation loved Steve (not his real name) and would always celebrate his gift when he spoke at various times during the year. Sometimes, it seemed, they celebrated a little too much…

One day, a ruthless self-talk session yielded in me the conscious decision to be Steve's greatest fan and resist any temptation to be intimidated by or insecure in the presence of his God-given calling and ability. This battle fought and won internally also had to find external expression. So, when Steve would do pulpit ministry, I would always follow his message with great accolades of appreciation (not contrived but genuine) and would be the first to contribute to special love offerings received for him after special seasons of his sacrificial ministry to the congregation.

I will never forget the evening after one of those special services when Steve preached that an elder in the church pulled me over to the side and asked to have a word with me. Having no idea what the subject of the conversation would be, I followed this elder into an area where we could have a semi-private moment and intently listened as he spoke. While I do not remember the exact words he used, his essential message went something like: "Pastor, I cannot express to you how much we all appreciate the way you treat Steve and lift him up when he ministers. In case you didn't know, we respect your leadership even more because of your willingness to 'let him shine'".

It was at that moment long ago that, by the grace of God, a major potential enemy in me took flight. I have since seen this enemy strangle the potential of many churches and other organizations where gifted and talented people sit anxiously awaiting the opportunity to be involved in significant ways but who are frustrated because of the invisible but very real monster of INSECURITY in leaders around them.

Back to the Garden

Sin's effect reached deeper than many realize and is always the culprit, in one way or the other, behind dysfunctions in human relationships. As one rereads the biblical narrative in Genesis 3-4, it becomes obvious that sin affects our relationships with God, others, and even with ourselves. The redemptive work of Christ touches all of those areas, but we are all on a journey and are "works in progress."

One of the eventual fruits of the sin-dysfunction was the murder of Abel by Cain, and thus the desire to subdue the influence of others to make ourselves look better became a part of the human dilemma. It is interesting to note the prevalence of this problem in Jehoram, Abijah, and Athaliah's reigns.

Insecurity Portrayed

The spirit of insecurity and corresponding acts of violence and murder are prominent in Jehoram and Athaliah's narratives. From the narrative, murderous activities do not seem to have been a part of Abijah's practice. However, it is interesting that his short reign of only one year did not serve to provide a turnaround from the acts of his father and predecessor, Jehoram. Neither did his short monarchy prevent in any way the despicable behavior of his mother and successor, Athaliah.

Jehoram is a prime example of how some leaders are resentful rather than grateful for the strong and gifted people. Once established in his position, one of the first agenda items for this notorious leader was his brothers' actual murder! While certainly filled with a great deal of irony and contempt, Elijah's letter the prophet sent to this king is revelatory on several fronts. Not the least of these gaffs from the prophet toward the king was the stinging rebuke stating that the murdered siblings had been "men who were better than you" (2 Chron. 21:13b, NIV).

Whether this perspective of the brothers of Jehoram is true or just an exaggeration for emphasis by the man of God, what is certain is that the king murdered these brothers out or a sense of insecurity and feeling threatened for his position and power. Establishing a very effective "team" to benefit the kingdom may have resulted if only Jehoram would have incorporated and utilized the brothers' talents rather than snuffing those out for self-promotion!

Athaliah was a real "piece of work." Having already negatively influenced (from God's perspective!) the reigns of both her husband (Jehoram) and son (Abijah), she proceeds to do the unspeakable when taking over the throne after Abijah's death. The wicked queen, another clear portrait of the cruel and vicious nature of insecurity, proceeds to eliminate her family, including grandchildren, to wipe away any competition for the monarch position. Being a grandfather myself and observing my wife's love and treatment for our grandchildren, this story is especially impactful in illustrating the devilish results of insecurity when left unchallenged and unchecked.

It is also significant to note the actual "insanity" of insecurity revealed in Athaliah's murderous plan. She was potentially canceling her very own legacy by killing those who would come behind her! Had another family member not put themselves in danger to rescue one young grandson (Joash), the lineage of the kings that followed could have been drastically affected.

Insecurity Revealed

Many articles and books are available related to tell-tell signs of insecure leadership. With the relatively limited space in this chapter, I have chosen to make my list (an acrostic) from personal experiences and observations. While offered primarily for self-leadership purposes, please understand that the characteristics listed below should serve us well in recognizing, resisting, and restructuring as needed. There is no condemnation implied but only a total dependence on the grace of God to help us all overcome day by day!

I – IMAGE-DRIVEN

Leaders with extreme insecurities tend to emphasize one's image as related to substance and reality. One need only to look at King Saul's negative transformation to see this problem brought on early by pride but developing into insecurity and corresponding paranoia. In 1 Samuel 15, we see Saul being rejected by God and rebuked by Samuel, but more concerned about his image before the elders and the people than his verdict from God (1 Sam. 15:30)!

N – NEEDY

Insecure leaders often show signs of co-dependency by becoming so needy of the approval and accolades of others that they become affirmation-addicts. Whatever gets applause, draws a crowd, causes the cameras to flash, makes the coffers run over, etc., are within bounds for the affirmation-addict.

S – SACRIFICE

Sacrifice is often a very admirable term when used to describe leaders and a leadership culture. However, in this section, the term refers to a leader's willingness to sacrifice their organization's well-being as long as their recognition and reputation are growing. When this manifestation of insecurity is operative, organizational budgets, staff, properties, etc., tend to be considered by the leader as personal assets and are used (sometimes used up!) to gain notoriety and networks for the leader's self-aggrandizement.

E - EGO-CENTRIC

How leaders communicate is often very revelatory as to the presence of insecurity. The frequent use of the first-person singular pronoun ("I") is obvious while, when discussing "wins" and positive outcomes, the use of the first-person plural ("we") or third person ("they") is often noticeably absent.

Also, insecurity can be present when a person (leader) is either continually finding fault with or playing the comparison game with other leaders and organizations in the community or feels the need to "one-up" anyone around them with bigger-and-better stories of personal or corporate exploits. While they may appear interested in what you are saying, they are planning an immediate segue from your story into their more "interesting" version! As the old-timers used to say, "Be careful not to steal someone else's thunder!"

C - CONTROL

Those insecure in their leadership have extreme difficulty delegating responsibility and providing success elements for that (resources, authority, feedback, etc.). Micromanaging is often the management style with outbursts of anger when things are slightly off track. Overbearing supervision produces a climate of fear where a lack of creativity and failure-aversion is prominent. Mistreatment of others "because we are doing God's business" is sometimes the language used to justify controlling through insecurity. Akin to this is also the unwillingness to promote/elevate others to places of greater influence.

These characteristics often result in a continual turnover of staff and a revolving door of volunteers and other constituents. High caliber, highly motivated, and greatly gifted people will not tolerate a controlling, insecure leader for more than a few months before they are finding another opportunity in another!

U – UNABLE

Insecurity brings with it a certain filter for information and makes receiving genuine feedback almost impossible. Leaders tend to allow only information that affirms an already preconceived idea and reinforces a plan/behavior already in motion. When information perceived as negative by the leadership needs sharing, the messengers are noticeably scarce! Additionally, when challenged over suggestions made, leader insecurity will have an immediate and automatic reaction of "personal affront." In other words, insecure leaders are very sensitive and take everything personally!

The same leaders who are feedback and challenge resistant are often quite ready to practice a feedback style themselves that is less than profitable. Constituents come to dread the "Seagull Management Style" (term borrowed from a lecture by Ken Blanchard) style that characterizes the context: 1) the leader swoops down quickly; 2) dumps on everybody, and then 3) flies away!

R – RESIST

Often an insecure leader is so overly committed to the organizational task to the point of working themselves into a place of exhaustion and numbness. Trusting others and releasing the work to others (even for a few days!) while needed rejuvenation is received is resisted because "this thing might fall apart if I'm not here." While a good work ethic is admirable and is a component of any good leadership effort, it is always ultimately destructive when one's position and performance are the primary determinants of personal worth and security. Just because the job title may be "pastor" does not exempt the leader from this tendency and danger.

Insecure leaders caught in this never-ending, ever-accelerating hamster wheel existence will consistently resist the need to slow down for personal self-care (physical, emotional, relational, and spiritual, etc.). This resistance will even sometimes be spiritualized and projected on others ("I haven't had a day off in months, so why should you not do the same?") and will eventually result in that leader's effectiveness grinding to a screeching halt with others asking, "What happened to them?"

E – ELEVATE

While this final characteristic, elevate, could perhaps be incorporated into some of the ones already mentioned, it serves us well to end this chapter with the simple reminder that leadership is about lifting others and assisting them in fulfilling their God-given design and destiny! Our job is to help elevate others through encouragement, training, opportunities, discovery, etc., and to do so with a heart that celebrates their ascendency into places and positions that even "outrun" us. Insecure leaders have real problems seeing their purpose as one of assisting others in succeeding!

And… I think this means not "killing" those around you who may look like threats to your position!

Chapter Five – King Jehoash (Joash) (835-796) 2 Kings 12; 2 Chronicles 23-24

Jehoash's name means "Yahweh has given." Indeed, he had been given life. He survived the purge of his grandmother. Spared from her murderous rampage, Jehoash became the sole survivor. His reign began at the young age of seven and continued for 40 years. This four-decade time span can be divided into descriptive periods.

1. The Period of Following

As covered in the previous chapter, Jehoash's paternal aunt, Jehosheba, saved his life when he was a mere one-year-old. Her husband, Jehoiada, faithfully led the nation as the high priest. Together, they and many others ensured the safe hiding of Jehoash until he reached the tender age of seven. They ensured his coronation at the earliest possible point.

For many years, it is likely that Jehoiada led the nation of Judah. During this important transitional season, numerous urgent items were completed. They eliminated the wicked Queen Athaliah in the coup. They destroyed the Baal temple along with Mattan, the Baal priest. Baalism, with its immoral and human sacrifices, was ended. They led the nation in renewing the covenant.

Finally, the Jewish temple had fallen into disrepair. Athaliah had even used the sacred objects from the Jewish temple in the temple to Baal. Financial steps were initiated to raise all the capital funds needed for repairs.

During these early years, the biblical text gives Jehoash's name as the leader. Nevertheless, Jehoiada served as the great influencer. He carefully chose two wives for Jehoash. The royal line had to be restored, but the past history with large harems proved disastrous.

Jehoiada seemed cognizant of this danger. As a compliment to Jehoiada, he appeared in the background and let Jehoash receive the credit for these wise decisions. The period that followed were good years for the nation.

2. The Period of Growing

In the twenty third year of King Jehoash's reign, he reached the age of 30. At this time, the king became aware that the funds that had been raised for many years had not been fully implemented for the temple repairs. Perhaps Jehoiada's advanced age fostered some of the delays. Regardless, the young king took his own positive initiatives, even over Jehoiada and all the priests. He ensured the temple was restored to its original beauty and further strengthened its operations. This period of growth was good years for the nation.

3. The Period of Forsaking

At an advanced age, Jehoiada the priest died. Out of immense respect for his countless contributions, a grateful nation had the venerated priest buried with the Judean kings in the city of David. An ominous description had been made earlier in the text about king Jehoash, "He did what was right all the days of Jehoiada the priest." Those good old days had now come to an end. The days of the new beginning days would not be good.

Sometime after the death of Jehoiada, the corrupt officials of Judah approached king Jehoash with terrible counsel. They urged the king to consider serving the Canaanite fertility goddess Asherah. The pagan religious practices were often accompanied with vile, immoral events and child sacrifice. Incredibly, the young king yielded to their requests and went wayward. He abandoned the Jewish temple and embraced the Canaanite practices.

Numerous godly prophets admonished the king and leaders to return to the Lord. The scribe even made a reference to a written record of these many prophecies. Though the prophets testified correctly, the leaders did not listen. Jehoiada's own son, Zechariah, prophesied to the people. His message was, "You will not prosper. Because you have forsaken the Lord, he will forsake you."

Again, the people did not listen. Instead, a murderous plot arose from them. They managed to persuade King Jehoash to issue a capital offense against Zechariah. At the very courtyard where Zechariah's father, Jehoiada, had so graciously installed Jehoash as king, he now returned evil for good. Jehoash did not remember the kindness of Zechariah's father. He had Zechariah stoned. As the life was ebbing out of him, Zechariah declared, "May the Lord see this and call you to account." That prayer was heard.

4. The Period of Reaping

The biblical text links Jehoash's sowing of evil leadership with his reaping the oppression of the Syrian nation. The Judeans greatly outnumbered the Syrians, but hopelessly lost the battle to a smaller force. The bulk of the ungodly Judean leadership were killed by the Syrians. Even King Jehoash was left severely wounded. He was required to surrender all the gold of the royal and sacred treasuries to persuade the withdrawal of the attack.

Eventually, Jehoash was killed by his own servants while he was recovering at the palace area. The innocent blood of Zechariah, the son of Jehoiada, stirred the actions of Jehoash's servants to take revenge on him. One of the servants was the son of an Ammonite woman. The other servant was the son of a Moabite woman.

The Ammonites and Moabites were descended from Abraham's nephew, Lot. Many centuries earlier, Lot had displayed ungratefulness to his uncle with the choosing of the land. The symbolism of his descendants' killing of King Jehoash would not have been lost to the people of Judah. Even descendants of the ungrateful Lot could not tolerate Jehoash's level of ungratefulness to Jehoiada.

Conclusion on King Jehoash

The death of King Jehoash concludes with a despondent note. He was buried in Jerusalem, although he was "not buried in the royal tombs of the kings." In other words, he may have had the title of nobility, but his actions were anything but noble. He had good advisors in his youth, but sadly yielded to bad advisors.

Application - Chapter Five - Jehoash (Joash) - Helping a Kid Be a King

At the time of this writing, the United States and the entire world are still reeling from the effects of the COVID 19 virus's invasion and its impact on individuals, families, businesses, institutions, and other societal entities and concerns. Nothing has been left untouched, but, thankfully, some definitive paths forward are beginning to emerge, and hope seems to be rising as to how this challenge might become the catalyst for some very positive changes!

Amidst the many sad stories that have emerged because of COVID, some lighter moments have served well to help navigate the times. The very entertaining (because it did not end in tragedy!) story of a five-year-old boy named Adrian Zamarrippa[29] is an example of this and will surely bring a smile.

Adrian was undoubtedly suffering from "cabin fever" induced by the social distancing restrictions and in-home seclusions brought on by prolonged issues with the coronavirus. While the lack of socializing and constantly being confined takes its toll on adults, this proves to be especially hard on children. Therefore, Adrian takes advantage of his sixteen-year-old babysitting sister's nap, removes the keys to his parent's SUV from the key holder in the kitchen, stuffs his pocket with three dollars from his piggy bank, and heads out toward Los Angeles to buy a Lamborghini! Adrian unbelievably traveled about three miles down Interstate 15 at the blazing speed of 32 miles per hour before a police officer spotted and stopped the vehicle and, thankfully before any serious problems arose. According to the referenced article from The Washington Post:

> Trooper Rick Morgan, the officer who pulled over Adrian, initially thought that he was an impaired driver, slumped down in his seat, said Lt. Nick Street, a public information officer for the Utah Highway Patrol.
>
> "He thought that maybe somebody was having a medical incident like cardiac arrest," said Street. "He was not prepared for who he saw in the driver's seat. [Adrian] was seated clear up to the edge of his seat, holding the steering wheel, and he had both feet on the brake pedal. The kid was extremely lucky that neither he nor anybody else got hurt."

Adrian was safely delivered back home, where his frantic parents and sister, though quite embarrassed and angry, welcomed him with open and grateful arms! As a post-note to the harrowing incident, a local entrepreneur, Jeremy Neves, heard of the incident and later showed up in his actual Lamborghini to give both Adrian and his family a ride around the community. Quoting the Post article once again:

> Education and discipline are certainly appropriate in Adrian's case, Neves said.
>
> "But please, let's not just focus on the bad," he said. "Let's not miss the gift and the genius of this little boy. He was determined, willing to do whatever it took to go after his dream. You don't want that dreaming to stop."

Even someone with big dreams and kingly potential desperately needs direction, proper training, and significant oversight to keep their dreams on track. Enter Joash…

Desire and Need for Mentoring

When reflecting on King Joash's life, the true but unsung hero in this story is the older priest, Jehoiada. Without his willingness to courageously squelch the evil reign of Queen Athaliah and replace her with the boy-king, Joash, things could have been quite different at that stage of Judean history. Jehoiada knew Joash was certainly not capable of ruling as a seven-year-old. He was also willing to take on the role of mentoring this young boy into a king that, at least for a time, would bring much-needed change to the spiritual climate of the nation.

While mentors actively influence many of the Judean kings and Joash's persons and practices, advising those either in leadership or preparing for leadership is prominent in other biblical stories.

Examples of Mentoring in Scripture

The Bible is replete with instances of mentoring. This practice, interwoven throughout the pages of scripture, is prominent in various leaders' lives navigating critical times in the history of God's dealings with His people. Some examples from both the Old and New Testament narratives include Moses and Joshua, David and Solomon, Paul and Timothy, and Jesus and the Twelve.

The interaction of Moses (mentor) and Joshua (protégé) during the sojourning of Israel through the wilderness and into the promised land of Canaan provides an important example of the mentoring process. Joshua follows his mentor into conflict situations (Exodus 17:8-16), going ahead of his mentor to access opportunities and challenges (Numbers 13:16-25), standing firm to the leader/mentor's vision amid opposition (Numbers 14:6-9), and eventually succeeding his mentor as leader over Israel (Numbers 27:18-23; Joshua 1:1-18). Joshua eventually completed Moses's vision to lead the people into Canaan and give them an inheritance (Joshua 8-19).

Another pivotal point in Israel's history was King David's monarchial transition to Solomon, his son (1 Kings 1:5-53). Mentoring is evident as David makes human and financial resources available for Solomon, his son and protégé, to accomplish visionary pursuits (1 Chronicles 22:1-19). This father/king/mentor also protects his protégé from adversarial competitors (1 Kings 1:5-30), both privately and publicly affirms Solomon as his successor (1 Kings 1:28-40) and gives detailed instructions to his protégé regarding organizational relationships and futures affairs of the kingdom (1 Kings 2:1-9). The goal of kingdom establishment and temple construction was a multi-generational task expedited by the practice of mentoring.

The Apostle Paul and Timothy's relationship, his protégé, provides a prominent illustration of mentoring in New Testament times. The relationship between Timothy and Paul involved a variety of situations, including traveling companion (Acts 16:1-3; 18:5), son in the faith (1 Timothy 1:2), fellow preacher and church leader (2 Corinthians 1:19; 1 Timothy 4:6-5:25), trusted emissary (Philippians 2:19-23), disciplined learner (2 Timothy 1:13-14; 2:1-2; 3:14-16), and faithful friend (2 Timothy 4:9-16). The final letter recorded in scripture from Paul's pen (2 Timothy) is addressed to Timothy, indicating the depth of love and measure of confidence this great mentor had towards his valued protégé.

Any overview of biblical examples of mentoring would be incomplete without emphasizing the quintessential mentor, Jesus Christ. All four gospel accounts (Matthew, Mark, Luke, and John) elucidate the purpose of Jesus as proclaiming, performing, and propagating the present reality of the Kingdom of God (Matthew 4:17; Mark 1:14-15; Luke 4:43; Luke 9:1-2; Luke 11:20; John 3:3). The propagation aspect was accomplished initially and primarily through the intentional mentoring by Jesus of the original, hand-selected twelve disciples (Mark 3:13-19).

Malphurs and Mancini offer helpful insight when dividing the leadership mentoring process of Jesus and the Twelve into four related but progressive steps.[30] Step one involves <u>recruiting</u> potential protégés by receiving those who sought him out (John 1:35-40) and the active pursuit of followers by mentor initiative (John 1:43; Mark 1:16-19). Commenting on the significance of this step, the authors declare, "If we are to shape leaders, we have little choice but to involve ourselves in the leadership recruitment business."[31]

Following the recruitment stage is step two, the prayerful selection of individuals recognized to have the qualities necessary for protégé success. Jesus modeled great intentionality in this step by spending all night in prayer before selecting the Twelve (Luke 6:12-16). He also was careful to provide revelatory opportunities relative to prospective learners' propensities towards initiative and obedience (Luke 5:1-11). Malphurs and Mancini again accentuate the importance of the selection step by proclaiming, "Each time Jesus selected a disciple, nothing was left to happenstance. He selected disciples with intention, for he had present and future plans for them."[32]

Step three in the mentoring process of Jesus consists of the actual training component. "Though Jesus ministered to the crowd, he focused on and trained the core...Jesus committed his life to the Twelve because he knew that they, not the crowd, would make a difference that would have eternal consequences."[33] The master mentor spent extended periods of time with his closest followers in secluded and intense teaching times (Matthew 5-7; Luke 6:20-49) and refused to send his followers on a mission before significant instruction (Matthew 10:5-42).

The final of the four steps discussed by Malphurs and Mancini is that of deployment. It is important to understand Jesus did perceive mentoring as something to be fully accomplished in a sterile classroom-type setting. He allowed for was insistent that his protégés exercise the opportunity to receive hands-on experience (Mark 6:7-13). Furthermore, mentoring Jesus-style included diligence in taking the time and effort to further train through debriefing after tasks were completed (Luke 10:17-20). The commission to reach the world with the gospel was a task that involved those willing to mentor others to maturity and kingdom effectiveness (Matthew 28:18-20)!

Mentoring was a powerful leadership force in biblical times and continues to be so today!

Not Optional Equipment

One thing that is obvious when talking with people headed toward leadership in the 21st century is the expectation of ongoing mentorship, both personally and professionally. In recent years, the "life coach" movement has exploded, thus indicating the desire and felt-need for continued improvement among people from most any walk-of-life and vocational context. This trend is a very encouraging phenomenon that leaders must consider when attempting to posture their organizations with strong leadership for the future. While the terms mentor, coach, counselor, advisor, etc., have different nuances of meaning, the essence of all of these is the interaction of one person in another's life to help that person become all they were "Divinely designed" to be. In the case of Joash, it was "helping a kid be a king."

In order, however, for a mentoring endeavor to be successful, there must be complementary forces at work in both the mentor and the protégé. The protégé must desire the assistance and honest feedback of the mentor. Complementing this, the mentor must enter the relationship with a positive perspective of the trainees' potential to learn and grow. While Jehoiada and Joash's historical context entered different factors into their leadership paradigm, Jehoiada would never have gone to the lengths to posture Joash for the throne had he not been convinced of the seven-year-old's potential to eventually lead the kingdom well.

A Leader's Perspective of Others

Two very interesting concepts arising several years ago in organizational leadership studies help shed some light on the importance of leaders' perspective and the impact that has on the commitment, loyalty, competence, and overall effectiveness of organizational constituents. While space does not allow for any detailed discussion of these ideas here, a brief overview can suffice at this point.

In the 1950s-60s, researcher Douglas McGregor provided some important insight as to how leaders tend to lead others relative to the overall expectations of the people's motivation level and work ethic. Characterizing workers into the two general categories of Theory X and Theory Y, MacGregor expounds on different practices and approaches taken by leaders as they attempt to access the workforce and adapt management styles accordingly in order to bring the greatest productivity.[34]

Others have popularized similar studies under the moniker of the "Pygmalion Effect." This concept is yet another attempt to express to leaders how important the perspectives of those working with them are. These perspectives have a significant impact on the expectations and approaches they bring to workplace interaction with others. An earlier article by J. Sterling Livingston referenced in the January 2003 volume of the Harvard Business Review provides a brief but enlightening explanation of the Pygmalion name and principle:

> J. Sterling Livingston named this 1969 article after the mythical sculptor who carves a statue of a woman brought to life. His title also pays homage to George Bernard Shaw, whose play *Pygmalion* explores the notion that the way one person treats another can, for better or worse, be transforming. In his article, Livingston notes that creating positive expectations is remarkably difficult. He offers managerial guidelines: Focus special attention on expectations set during an employee's first year, make sure new hires get matched with outstanding supervisors, and set high expectations for yourself.[35]

What we gather from these brief overviews is simple confirmation that one of the major determinates in helping to mentor someone to a place of greater personal and professional effectiveness is the attitude and approach of the mentor to the protégé. To put it in "Jehoiada" terms, "If you never see a 'king in the kid,' you will rarely see the 'kid become the king.'"

A Disclaimer

As Jehoiada and Joash's relationship has allowed us some insights into the importance of mentoring, both then and now, a disclaimer is in order as this chapter is concluding.

One will notice that Jehoiada believed in and invested heavily in the boy-king Joash and that King Joash did well for years. King Joash brought a certain sense of revival and spiritual renewal to Judah that appears to have lasted for quite a few years. Eventually, however, after the death of Jehoiada, King Joash reverted to idolatry practices and even stooped so low as to have the sons of Jehoiada killed. Murdered by his servants (men from Ammon and Moab) and not even permitted burial in the kings' tombs, the reign of King Joash, the boy-turned-king, ended in disgrace.

When one serves in a mentoring capacity, whether as an executive trainer, Pastor, parent, corporate coach, teacher, etc., it is hugely important to understand that good training does not guarantee forever-good results. While it is a privilege to be a leader and mentor sowing into others, one must still realize only God is ultimately in control of the results. Be encouraged that seeing the potential in others and helping them discover, develop, and deploy that potential is honorable and a primary focus of Godly leaders. Plant that good seed, cultivate those young and vibrant plants, and be not weary in well-doing. God will bring the increase!

Even if it is not a Lamborghini!

Chapter Six – King Amaziah - (796-767) 2 Kings 14; 2 Chronicles 25

The writers of 2 Kings and 2 Chronicles compliment King Amaziah, but with some criticisms. At the age of 25, he assumed the leadership of Judah. He reigned for 29 years; however, many of those years included the co-regency of his son, Uzziah. The reign of King Amaziah can be viewed from past, present, and future perspectives.

1. The Past Assassins

Amaziah inherited a past assassination of his father that needed to be addressed. In the previous chapter, we covered the fact that king Jehoash of Judah was assassinated by two of his servants. To King Amaziah's credit, he chose to bring the two guilty men to justice, while not exceeding the confines of Jewish law. The law clearly states, "Fathers shall not be put to death for their children, nor shall children be put to death for their fathers; a person shall be put to death for his own sin" (Deut. 24:6). Amaziah enacted justice against the murderers but permitted their children to live in line with Mosaic law. In our past view of the assassins, Amaziah displayed the healthy balance between justice and restraint.

2. The Present Mercenaries

The narrative quickly introduced a situation with hired mercenaries from Israel. Amaziah had already spent a staggering sum of money employing the mercenaries to assist in retaking the Edomite region. He hoped to regain the lucrative trade routes previously lost by his great-grandfather, Jehoram.

Into this present situation, an unnamed prophetic admonished the king to send the Israelite troops back home. Israel was a strongly idolatrous nation, and an alliance with them in battle would bring certain defeat. Naturally, Amaziah inquired about the potential loss of such a massive sum to the mercenaries. The prophet reassuringly replied, "The Lord can give you much more than that."

To King Amaziah's credit, he yielded to the prophet and sent the mercenaries home, much to their annoyance. On their return, they attacked and looted a number of Judean towns. Nevertheless, in our present view with the mercenaries, Amaziah displayed faith in the face of a difficult choice.

3. The Future Combatants

The prophet's positive prediction came to pass. Amaziah's sacrificial obedience to the command produced a decisive victory over the Edomites. The unique intersection of the trade routes would indeed give king Amaziah and Judah much more than they lost with the Israelite mercenaries. Great dangers often lurk near great victories. Amaziah would woefully fail the next two tests.

First, his men encountered the false idols that the Edomites worshipped. One would think a grateful king would destroy the idols. Incredibly, Amaziah brought the idols back to Judah, set them up as his gods, bowed down to them, and burned sacrifices to them. Unsurprisingly, an unnamed prophet corrected the king, but to no avail. Amaziah did not listen. Therefore, the prophet predicted that destruction lay ahead.

Second, the victory of the Edomites went to the young king's head. He challenged the northern king Jehoash (not to be confused with Amaziah's father, who is also named Jehoash) to a battle. A stele erected by the Assyrian king Adad-nirari III mentioned "Jehoash the Samaritan."[36] Amaziah most likely hoped to recover the lost mercenaries' payment and the damage they had inflicted.

Though Jehoash warned Amaziah to cease his wrong-headed attack, the warning went unheeded. King Jehoash's army soundly defeated Amaziah's army. The Israelites took treasure from the palace and the temple. They tore down a 600-foot section in the Jerusalem walls, leaving the city defenseless. They also took hostages captive, including King Amaziah himself. The cocky king now humbly went to prison. In our future view with combatants, Amaziah failed.

Conclusion on King Amaziah

Eventually, Amaziah was released from captivity. Like his father Jehoash of Judah, he began well but did not end well. Also, he too became the victim of an assassination. A coup arose in Jerusalem, but Amaziah fled to Lachish for safety. The assassins pursued him to Lachish, killed him, and returned his body to Jerusalem to be buried with the kings. The root cause of the conspiracy may have stemmed from Amaziah bringing such dire disasters upon Judah.

Amaziah's name means "strengthened by Yahweh." When he followed good directions, he did receive Yahweh's strength. Sadly, he forsook the correct path, trusted in his own strength, and made disastrous decisions. His army was defeated. His riches were gone. His power was gone. In the end, he died a very weak leader.

Application - Chapter 6 - Amaziah - Strength in Rest

It was years ago, I have long forgotten her name, but her tearful voice is a memory that remains.

In our high school science class, she entered late, distraught, and drawing the teacher's attention. As memory serves, the conversation between this teenage girl and the teacher proceeded:

Teacher: What's wrong? Why are you crying?

Student: My dad is going to kill me! I ruined my car!

Teacher: What happened to your car?

Student: The tow truck guy said I destroyed the engine… no oil!

Teacher: Was the oil warning light on?

Student: Yes. (Sobbing stronger now)

Teacher: How long has the light been on?

Student: Two weeks!

To his credit, the teacher stopped the conversation lest he adds insult to injury through the painful reminder that warning lights are there for a reason: stop now and address the problem!

It is always dangerous to ignore warning signals given as a reminder of the designer's prescribed limits! I certainly hope my high school classmate learned a good life lesson and that things turned out well between her and her dad.

When ignoring instructions for proper function and successful operation, one may not only have to deal with a malfunctioning automobile but may even find their life and leadership broken down with no vitality to move forward. However, this is not God's will or desire for any of His people.

Strengthened by Yahweh

The name Amaziah, "strengthened by Yahweh," is a very powerful reminder of both the necessity and source of strength available to one leading from a God-centric perspective. However, the promise is always only as good as the potential recipient's willingness to meet the conditions set forth.

Strength promised from the LORD to Amaziah, and many other kings both before and after him, was contingent on the exercise of an unwavering trust in God's providence and provision. This trust is necessary even when circumstances were screaming otherwise. Amaziah ultimately succumbed to the pressures of conformity, intimidation, and expectations of societal forces around him. Like several other kings both before and after him, he refused to follow God's prescribed way of "trust and obey" and brought upon himself a very sad and tragic end.

The good news is that "strength from Yahweh" is still available for those who will trust His promises AND His prescribed practices. The bad news is that many Christ-centered leaders in the driven-ness, results-oriented 21st-century organizational climate neglect some God-designed practices that will usher in the promise of strength and longevity. One of the most neglected of these practices/disciplines is that of consistent rest and Sabbath-keeping.

God Actually Did That

When God fashioned humankind on the sixth day of creation (Gen. 1:26-30), He did so with great intentionality and instructions for success. One of those specifications for humankind from the "Creator's Manual" was the necessity of rest. Rest was so significant in that scenario that it is much more than a precept. It is modeled for us by the Creator Himself. Humankind was to recognize rest as a part of creation's life-rhythm and are shown how to by the designer's own example!

While there are many considerations related to the reception and representation of the imago Dei, none may be more important in our present society than the regular exercise of intentional rest. In his book *Subversive Sabbath*, A. J. Swoboda offers an excellent overview of how the creation narrative illuminates rest as a gift from God. Swoboda emphasizes the powerful realization that the seventh day, God's rest day, was the first full day experienced by humankind, and thus "Adam and Eve's first full day of existence was a day of rest, not work."[37] It is also interesting to note the structure of creation "days" as beginning in the evening (e.g., "and the evening and the morning were the first day…" Gen. 1:5b). It seems God wants even our days to start focusing on rest to equip us for the work ahead!

When the commandment of a regularly observed Sabbath shows up in the Ten Commandments (Ex. 20:8-11), this is not a new revelation but the codification of something God instituted at the beginning for the well-being of His creation. Its inclusion in the Commandments reinforces the importance of the practice for all, yes, even those in pastoral ministry![38]

Jesus Actually Meant That

While a weekly day of rest applies to everyone, a group often overly susceptible to disobedience (yes, that is what it is!) to the Sabbath command are those in pastoral ministry or other ministry-focused endeavors. While not permissible, it is understandable how this group of well-meaning servants, called to help people in difficult life issues, have trouble entering into relaxation and true rest. However, Jesus both sets the example and speaks into this quite clearly.

In His final hours on earth with the cross looming, Jesus makes a statement that should cause us to listen intently. He declares in the prayer of John 17, "I have finished the work you have called me to do" (vs. 4). Are you serious, Jesus? How could you say this when, within a two-mile radius of where you are praying, there are many sick people, broken homes, dying addicts, hell-bound unbelievers, etc.? How could it be that you have finished what you came to do? The answer to these questions uncovers the secret to enjoying the gift of rest while swimming in the deep waters of human suffering: the understanding of calling and assignment.

No individual can be expected and called to do everything, and none of us can fulfill the Great Commission simply by "working a little harder" and ignoring time to rejuvenate. Our callings and assignments to a particular arena of service never include getting everything done. Our assignment is to work hard in our sphere of influence while taking ample time (per God's instructions) to rest consistently and thus to resist the devil's plot to "take us out early." What a joyful life-rhythm results when a pastor/leader sleeps well at night knowing that "I have finished the work you have called ME to do TODAY." What a joy a day off every seven days brings when one can declare, "I have finished the work you have called ME to do this WEEK." Moreover, how incredibly refreshing a vacation becomes when one realizes, "I have finished the work you have called ME to do this YEAR."

Jesus does not call people into the Kingdom Harvest to destroy them but promises rest to those "laboring and burdened down" (Matt. 11:28-30).

We Can Actually Do That

Okay… I hear some saying, "It is one thing to know God has established rest and another to recognize Jesus has promised rest, but it is a whole different thing to implement this in my situation."

Space here does not allow much discussion related to the implementation of good rest-rhythms (particularly if the well-meaning but mistaken mindset has influenced/infected you into thinking there is something "spiritual" about, "I haven't had a day off in months" or "I haven't taken a vacation in years!"). However, the following three disciplines borrowed from Pastor Rick Warren,[39] if scheduled and executed with great intentionality, can be a great start in training both we and others toward obedience to He who is both the Lord of the harvest and the Lord of the Sabbath.

Divert Daily

Finding rest begins with the daily discipline of healthy diversion. With unending responsibilities and expectations in focus each day, the willingness to unwind for a few minutes at a time is critical. Suzanna Wesley, mother of Charles and John Wesley, would reportedly find diversion and devotional time by setting a chair in the middle of the kitchen, pulling her apron over her head for a few minutes, and instructing her ten children not to interrupt during those sacred getaways! Students at the university that pass me walking from one building to another are not offended if I fail to acknowledge them.

They know I am diverting with a "five-minute vacation" and did not even "see" them come by!

Whatever your context allows, be very diligent in taking periodic "fresh air" spaces several times a day in order to divert with purpose.

Withdraw weekly

Our brief overview earlier of God's plan for humankind accentuated His one-day-out-of-seven design for the rhythm of rest to accompany a strong work ethic. While attempting not to be legalistic, this gift of rest does appear to entail 24 hours of uninterrupted restorative activity. Of course, Sunday is NOT that day for those in pastoral ministry!

What day of the week do you use for rest (restoration)? Is it a consistent calendar-marked day every week? Do others know this day is set apart (sanctified) for purposes outside of ministry activities and work-related events? Does your spouse know this day is set apart each week and look forward to it with/for you? Do you find yourself able to navigate difficult days more easily during the week because you know that day is coming? These are just some of the questions that we need to ponder when deciding to be diligent about God's command for self-restoration.

Abandon annually

Finally, the triumvirate of survival includes discipline on an annual basis; yes, a real vacation! Again, while not being legalistic about specifics, it appears that a relatively extended timeframe (no less than 7-10 days) is necessary to accomplish what annual vacations can provide. It usually takes at least three days to decompress from normal work, another 4-5 days to relax and find some restoration, and then another 2-3 days to prepare for reengagement. In other words, a day or two periodically several times a year does NOT tend to provide what a true annual vacation can accomplish!

Churches and other organizations operating in 21st-century pressure-cooker environs will be well-served by second-level leaders (board members, council members, elders, deacons, etc.) that insist on senior leaders setting the example for all other constituents by taking a mandatory vacation every 12 months. This endeavor does not need to be an expensive arrangement but can be as simple as a "staycation" involving a change of pace with no work-related responsibilities, on-call or otherwise. This practice will go a long way in creating a culture where people enjoy being involved, stay engaged long term, and will prove a win-win situation!

Final Words

Rest is a gift instituted from creation, exemplified by Jesus, and promised to those that will commit to being "strengthened by Yahweh" by doing things Yahweh's way! King Amaziah missed this gift of grace by doing things his way. However, heeding the warning of his disobedience, we can face a world of continual activity, uncertain horizons, and inordinate expectations with a supernatural strength and grace that is sufficient. What a joy to serve a life-giving Savior!

By the way, check your oil...

Chapter Seven – King Uzziah (Azariah) - (791-739) 2 Kings 14-15; 2 Chronicles 26

The record in 2 Kings uses the name of Azariah, which perhaps served as his throne name. In his annals, the Assyrian king, Tiglath-pileser III, made a reference to a king (spelled Azirau) who fits our king Azariah's timeframe and narrative.[40] Another Assyrian fragment references a possible Azariah of Judah (spelled Azirau of Iadau).[41] However, some debate remains if these references are to our king Azariah of Judah in this chapter. The name of Azariah means "Yahweh gives aid or success."

The 2 Chronicles' record uses the name of Uzziah, which perhaps was his original birth name. The prophets Amos, Hosea, Isaiah, and others consistently employ the name, Uzziah. Two seals with "servants of Uzziah" have also been discovered and published.[42] His name means "Yahweh gives strength." His reign can be divided into two main phases.

1. His Humility

Our narrative does not begin with the diligent efforts and great accomplishments of king Uzziah. Instead, we begin with his humility, which proved to be the cornerstone of his future success. Further, we see that his humility found its source in "seeking the Lord," a frequent theme in 2 Chronicles.

Uzziah took the throne at the young age of 16. His mentor in his formative years was a man named Zechariah. We only know of Zechariah's mentorship, and that he faithfully instructed the young king in the fear of God. Our narrative of his reign begins with the powerful statement, "As long as he sought the Lord, God gave him success." In many respects the name Azariah (Yahweh gives success) applied to the king.

The years of Uzziah and his Israelite counterpart were the golden years of the two Jewish kingdoms. For several decades Assyria declined both economically and militarily. Both Judah and Israel expanded during this season. However, the text reminds us that it was God's blessing on Jehoshaphat's life that allowed him to expand his kingdom southward to Eilat, the port city on the Gulf of Aqaba. Equally, his realm spread both eastward and westward, conquering the Ammonites and the Philistines.

Tribute funds poured into Judah, and Uzziah used them wisely. He restored the damage done to Jerusalem from the days of his father Amaziah. The king vigorously refortified his nation's defenses by equipping the army and building new defensive towers and walls. He even engaged his most skilled men to invent cutting edge weapons that could propel arrows and stones.

Beyond military preparations, he also oversaw many agricultural projects. The digging of cisterns, planting of vineyards, and enlarging the farming in rural areas rightfully earned him the compliment, "he loved the soil." The land itself prospered under his leadership. So remarkable was the success, that twice the text informs us of "his fame spreading far and wide." Again, in many respects the name Azariah (Yahweh gives success) applied to the king.

2. His Pride

The prophet Amos referred to a major earthquake that occurred when Uzziah was king of Judah. So great was the earthquake that over two centuries later the prophet Zechariah referred back to it. Geologists have evidence of a massive earthquake from this timeframe that may have measured near 8.2 on the Richter scale.[43]

Besides a physical earthquake, a spiritual one also occurred in King Uzziah's life. Yahweh had indeed made him successful

(Azariah); however, the text added the pointed caveat, "until he became powerful." The seismic event that hammered his life, left lasting debris, and fell along the fault line of the king's pride.

Mosaic law had a strong separation of powers between kings and priests. No amount of royalty made a Judean king a priest (Num. 18). For many years, Uzziah adhered to this biblical mandate. Yet, the surrounding nations often blurred the lines between regal and priestly roles for their kings. Even Uzziah's northern contemporary, King Jeroboam II of Israel, enjoyed the status of both king and priest. Maybe the comparison with other kingdoms triggered his initial desire to be a priest. Whatever his seminal thoughts, Uzziah's pride became the fulcrum of his downfall.

Uzziah arrogantly went into the inner room of the temple to offer incense. The high priest, accompanied by 80 other priests, confronted the king. In times past, Uzziah had yielded to the wise instruction of his mentor Zechariah. Now, he yielded to no one. He only displayed anger. He sought honor for himself. Instead, he contracted leprosy on his forehead. The priests hurried to remove him from the temple. Once he became aware of the leprosy, even Uzziah eagerly left the temple. He feared his affliction.

Conclusion on King Uzziah

King Uzziah was banned from the temple and never visited it again. He never recovered from his leprosy. In fact, he had to live in quarantine the rest of his life. His son Jotham was installed as a co-regent with him. One theory is that the king used the name Azariah (Yahweh gives success) during the successful years of his reign as a throne name. After he contracted leprosy, he switched to his original birth name of Uzziah, which is a request for "Yahweh to strengthen." He certainly needed God's mercy and strength.

Upon his death, Uzziah was buried near the kings but in a separate location due to his illness. The abrupt conclusion to his life ends not with his many accomplishments during 52 years of ruling, but with "The people said: he is a leper."

In 1931, a tablet was discovered in Israel dating to the Second Temple period. The Aramaic reads, "Here were brought the bones of Uzziah, King of Judah. Not to be opened."[44] During the vast construction project of the Second Temple, the king's tomb must have been moved to a location outside the city. For centuries, his lonely grave eloquently spoke the truth that "God resists the proud but gives grace to the humble."

Application - Chapter 7 - Uzziah - Who's Next?

My typical morning routine usually starts quite a bit before daybreak. It contains the following three elements: 1) a good cup of coffee (or two!), 2) scripture study and meditation, and 3) a glancing at the news to overview the most recent headlines.

For the last few months, the general topic related to potential leadership transitions has captured most of the space available in the media outlets accessed. At the time of this writing, the United States is just days before a presidential election. Additionally, hearings are underway for the potential replacement of now-deceased Supreme Court Justice Ruth Bader Ginsberg (SCOTUS justice: August 1993 – September 2020). Several states are posturing for elections and potential upsets in various congressional and gubernatorial elections. Societal unrest, personality and politically charged dichotomies, and a general sense of distrust have made the already tricky selection and transition tasks perhaps more challenging than ever before.[45]

Political arenas are only one example of the contexts in which intense decisions of transition take place. Corporations, churches, educational institutions, and almost any entity involving human interaction and leadership constructs (official and unofficial) will experience seasons of change specifically related to a shift in leadership. These transitions are never easy and can be especially difficult when leaders in high-impact positions are involved!

Deciding or discovering "who's next," though critical and necessary, can also be quite unnerving…

King Uzziah's Death

One can only imagine the angst on the streets of Jerusalem as the word begins to circulate of King Uzziah's death. History records his death somewhere around 742 BC after a mostly illustrious reign of some fifty-two years (some of the initial years as co-regent with his father, Amaziah).

Because of the length and relative national prosperity during Uzziah's monarchy, Judean citizens could not help but wonder who would be next in line for the throne and the "what" that "who" would introduce to the kingdom. By now, they understood that "as goes the leader, so goes the nation." Transition in leadership could mean a new day of increased momentum and regional influence for the country. However, this may result in a downturn of spiritual emphasis and commitment ushering in compromise, ungodly confederacies, and God's corresponding judgment on the nation. A lot was at stake; the people knew it and must have been very anxious about the shift to come.

Significantly, Isaiah's call as prophet occurs against the backdrop of the uncertainty surrounding the death of Uzziah and the accompanying transition (Is. 6:1). It is also essential to see within that prophetic calling and the futuristic fog of apprehension surrounding it a strong vision of God on His throne and in control! It is as if the LORD says to Isaiah and all Judah that the palace's physical throne may be temporarily empty, but "Someone" still very much occupies the throne in heaven! The nation can rest on the heavenly king's power and sovereignty even when uneasy about the next earthly ruler's inauguration.

Resting on God's solid and everlasting foundation will always allow a sense of stability in leadership transitions and the "who's next" life situations. Whether experiencing a personal change or affected by other leaders' transition, a Christ-centered perspective can provide a potential climate of individual and organizational peace during the shift at hand.

Leadership Succession

The process of succession in a context like the Judean monarchy is quite different from most leadership contexts in the 21st-century experience. However, it is interesting to note, and as referred to in the earlier discussion of King Rehoboam (see chapter one), even the kingly succession within those ancient systems, was not always as cut-and-dry as one may think. Succession was sometimes not automatic relative to birth order but resulted from the astute observation of skills and intentional training of recognized talents.

The point here is that leadership succession is too important to depend on chance, the sometimes-tainted preferences of various stakeholders, or the pressures of an immediate need to fill a vacancy. Successful succession is the result of much effort, intentionality, planning, collaboration, and training. As is apparent, none of these are terms that imply a hurried decision but rather a process with specific goals in mind and benchmarks along the way!

When considering a succession plan to discover and develop the best "who's next" candidate(s), multifaceted aspects of the process sometimes hamper leaders from executing the needed construction and implementation. The adage is right in this regard when realizing "the journey of 1000 miles begins with the first step." The first step in "who's next" must be present leadership's willingness to admit limitations in their current roles. The possibility of promotion and a new assignment (a good thing!), physical mortality (the mortality rate is still 100%!), and eventual lack of role availability (no one will serve effectively in a role indefinitely) are all considerations in this regard. After settling this soul-searching reality check, the next step in "who's next" defines what should characterize those moving into successor preparation.

The Bible records one of the most well-known leadership succession stories related to a young shepherd from Bethlehem named David (1 Sam. 16:1-13). While David did not initially appear to have what others would have considered "kingly, leadership qualities," the scripture reminds all leaders that looking just on image and perceived potential from a human perspective can often lead to missing the most God-gifted and ordained around us (16:7). No doubt, Spiritual discernment is an essential tool when considering leadership succession. However, since the biblical narrative provides the inspection of David's story as a whole, there are also definite indicators that provide insight into what God saw in him that might not have been immediately visible to others. Hopefully, the overview of some of those potential leadership indicators helps us recognize some crucial characteristics of "who's next" candidates.

Leadership Potential – Observations from David's Life

a. Preconceptions:

Do not establish a long list of fixed preconceived notions of what characterizes leadership. This assumption was the problem that Samuel, Saul, and David's family had when God was ready to use him. While Goliath and even his brothers disdained him and Saul doubted him, God delighted in him!

b. Transition:

When God is through with something, do not hold on to it. Before God could use Samuel to go to Bethlehem to anoint the "who's next" for Israel, He first had to slightly rebuke the prophet for the inability to move on as the season had changed. "How long will you mourn for Saul…"

c. Discernment:

Though mentioned earlier, this bears repeating. Assessments and parameters established by human ingenuity and understanding have their place but must ultimately give precedence to the voice of the Spirit and faithful discernment.

d. Patience:

When the right choice does not immediately appear, wait until it does. Do not press through and appoint "just anyone" as the "who's next." Impatience in this scenario will often be the rich soil of bad fruit and deep regret. David was "last in line" as the brothers showed up for the job!

e. Process:

Observe potential leaders as they both respect and appreciate the "process." David went through years of a process as he "led" the lion, bear, giant, 400 men; 600 men; the tribe of Judah; and finally, the whole nation of Israel. From the time of his "anointing" (1 Sam. 16) to the time of his "appointing" (2 Sam. 5) was a long and often painful process of over 15 years!

f. Responsible:

After Samuel anointed David to be king, he then goes back to the fields to take care of sheep and the responsibilities at hand. How faithful are potential leaders in the jobs they presently have? How excellent is someone in doing "menial" tasks? Faithfulness in lesser things is a significant indicator related to the trust of greater responsibilities (Luke 16:10-12).

g. Authority:

Authority is a significant concern in upheaval and distrust as is being experienced in 21st-century society. David exemplifies the willingness to respect and honor authority over him. Whether in obedience to his father to take food to his brothers, in faithful service to a paranoid King Saul who was threatening his life, or even when refusing to speak against or harm Saul in any way as the "anointed" of God, David's regard for authority is evident and admirable. He knew how to live under authority on his way to having authority!

h. Convictions:

When facing Goliath (1 Sam. 16), the major difference between David and the soldiers in Israel's army was a firm conviction of the challenged values and the stakes connected to those ("is there not a cause..."). Others cowered when the intimidating circumstances outweighed the antagonism to the glory of God!

i. Maverick:

While David was respectful to Saul and others, he was not afraid to challenge the processes and parameters. Vain desire did not drive these departures from the conventional. Instead, these resulted from opportunities and challenges that required God's direction for success.

j. Praise:

When facing Goliath, the glory of God was at the forefront of his concerns. After defeating the Philistine opponent, it was still God's name that David insisted be lifted high and exalted. Throughout most of his life, this "Sweet Psalmist of Israel" prioritized praise to the Most High rather than self-adulation.

k. Self-aware:

David knew his strengths and was unwilling to move into an arena where his gifts were not appropriate or accepted. This reluctance is apparent when he chose to use "five smooth stones" rather than attempt to fight Goliath with the traditional array of military equipment, even the king's armor!

l. Risk-taking:

The aversion to risk-taking did not find a foothold in the mind and leadership of David. God could use him to move Israel forward to new levels because of his willingness to stretch outside of the comfort zone and face dangers and uncertainties ahead.

m. Perseverance:

This "who's next" leader in Israel was able to press through discouragement from others: disregard (Saul), derision (brothers), disdain (Goliath).

n. Retaliation:

David learned early the threat of jealousy from others and the necessity of resisting the ever-present temptation toward retaliation. He did not enter into a spear-throwing contest with Saul!

o. Resilience:

Unfortunately, one of the most remembered incidents in David's life was his series of failures (adultery, intrigue, murder, etc.), beginning with the adultery committed with Bathsheba (2 Sam. 11). At some point, David realized failure does not have to be final and submitted to the process of repentance and restoration before God.

p. Humility:

It appeared to some (as accusations from David's brothers indicate) that David was a mischievous and arrogant teenager wanting to make a name for himself at the battle with Goliath. However, this account's story and other incidences reveal David, not an arrogant punk enamored with youthful zeal and self-assurance, but utterly confident in the power of God working for Kingdom good.

q. Initiative:

When David went to fight Goliath, he ran toward the obstacle and challenge, not from it. Even today, the Israeli army talks about the "law of the first strike" when facing what appears to be a much greater foe. The willingness to be proactive rather than reactive when facing problems is critical!

r. Servanthood:

David's victory over Goliath resulted in the rest of Israel's army's motivation to move forward in battle engagement, the enemy's defeat, and the gathering of the spoils. Servant leaders' exercises "positive peer pressure" by setting an example that, when followed, will serve for the betterment and blessing of others.

Leadership Potential – Instructions from Paul's Final Letter

Paul's last letter, 2 Timothy, is hugely significant. Paul's realization of the brevity of time he has left on earth (2 Tim. 4:6-8) undoubtedly feeds the sense of urgency and types of instruction he gives to Timothy, his "son in the faith." Knowing this may very well be the last instructions he leaves for his protégé, Paul is motivated to reemphasize critical aspects of self-leadership for Timothy's benefit. Paul expounds on key issues related to the continued effective perpetuation of the gospel message and church expansion to provide strategic instruction for the younger minister.

Among the instructions for church expansion, the apostle provides Timothy with three powerful metaphors related to leadership succession. 2 Timothy 2:1-7 focuses on an ongoing construct of discipleship, mentoring, and leadership development as Paul instructs his son to "consider" characteristics of "faithful people" by observing good soldiers, competitive athletes, and hardworking farmers.

For the remainder of this chapter, we would like to allow you to take some time and personally "consider" (exercise the mind) these word pictures and what they mean to 21st-century leaders. Perhaps you and your team may want to consider some of the following questions together:

How might this instruction help us to recognize potential leadership trainees in the "who's next" considerations for our organization?

What perspectives and practices might characterize these metaphors collectively?

What characteristics might apply to these metaphors more specifically when considered individually?

What systems of observation, discovery, affirmation, and training might best serve our organizations in pipelining leaders to be ready for the "who's next" opportunities and responsibilities ahead?

How might local churches consider these issues in providing well-prepared "who's next" candidates for leadership both for and from the church?

Good soldiers:

Characteristics: Systems:

_____   _____

_____   _____

_____   _____

_____   _____

_____   _____

_____

Competitive athletes:

Characteristics: Systems:

_____   _____

_____   _____

_____   _____

_____   _____

_____   _____

Hardworking farmers:

Characteristics: Systems:

_____   _____

_____   _____

_____   _____

_____   _____

A Final Word

While leading the caravan of travelers down the road to effectiveness, it is undoubtedly vital to have a good view out the windshield (vision). It is also valuable to have good peripheral insight from both sides to stay aware of the surroundings (cultural factors). However, there is no greater insight than to keep one's eyes glancing in the rearview mirror to make sure there are some actually following and to ensure a "who's next" is in training to take over the lead when needed. It is never too early to start thinking beyond success and even significance and into succession!

Chapter Eight – King Jotham and Ahaz (Jehoahaz) – (750-715) 2 Kings 15-16; 2 Chr. 27-28

In this chapter we will combine the father and son kings of Jotham and Ahaz. Both had co-reigns with their fathers and their sons. Both have been uncovered in archaeology. A royal seal discovered in 1940 mentions Jotham and Ahaz. The seal now resides in the Yale Babylonian collection.[46] The bullah reads, "Belonging to Ahaz son of Jotham, King of Judah." An additional seal in the Moussaieff collection also contains a fingerprint, which may belong to Ahaz himself.[47]

Additionally, both kings had reigns of similar length; however, with dramatically different philosophies of leadership. We have placed both of these kings together to explore their contrasting leadership. In particular, we will compare these two kings in two major areas of leadership approaches.

1. Contrasts in Their Military Approach

King Jotham began his reign at the young age of 25 and served 16 years in his reign. He exercised diligence in defending his nation. He made needed repairs and refortifications. The narrative describes his successful subjugation of the Ammonites during his reign. Near this time, the prophet Amos condemned the Ammonites, "because they have ripped up the women with child" (Amos 1:13). The Ammonites are listed 123 times in the Bible and were frequent adversaries of the Judeans.

A statue of an Ammonite king was found in Jordan in the 1960s.[48] The names on the statue's base are most likely the son and grandson of the Ammonite king, Shanib, whom Jotham defeated. In 2010 another

Ammonite statue was rescued by archaeologists from a trash heap in Jordan with the same historical connections.[49]

Both Jotham and Ahaz faced a coalition of two nations that came up against them. King Pekah of Israel and King Rezin of Syria united their armies against Judah. Faced with such a great challenge, we see two approaches to the situation.

First, the biblical text states that Jotham fought against their combined forces. As a summary about his military approach, the text states, "Jotham grew powerful because he walked steadfastly before the Lord his God." The prophets Amos, Hosea, Micah, and Isaiah were contemporary with King Jotham and most likely gave him wise counsel.

Second, Ahaz panicked when he faced the same coalition of Israel and Syria. The prophet Isaiah encouraged him to hold steady, but to no avail. In the southeast, the Edomites rebelled against Ahaz and carried Jewish prisoners away. In the west, the Philistines captured key cities and Judah lost significant ground. Judah had heavy losses with the Syrians and the northern Israelites. To protect himself, Ahaz became a vassal of the Assyrians. Initially, everything appeared to work out. The Assyrians defeated Israel and Syria. The ruthless Assyrian king, Tiglath-Pileser III, recorded this event in his inscriptions.[50] He also mentioned Jehoahaz of Judah, along with his tribute money.[51] Eventually, the contract with the Assyrian king went wrong. Assyria became an oppressor to Judah.

2. Contrasts in Their Spiritual Approach

The succinct message of King Jotham's spiritual approach to leadership was, "He did what was right in the eyes of the Lord." His son, Ahaz, is a completely different story. Throughout all his military disasters, he doubled down on his wrong thinking. Since the surrounding nations defeated him, he reasoned that he should serve their gods. In a prolific fashion, he established places of pagan worship in every single city of Judah. He replaced the Jewish altar with an Assyrian one. Worst of all, he offered his sons in dedication to the god Moloch. The event could be either ceremonial, or in some cases a child sacrificial offering. He most likely did both over the years of his reign.

Conclusion on King Jotham and King Ahaz

Leadership, good or bad, can be measured in its impact upon the people. With Jotham, he remained faithful to God in spite of how some of his people continued their corrupt practices. He lived right and led well. Ultimately, the people respected Jotham. They buried their king in the royal tombs. On the other hand, Ahab made his people's lives more difficult. The scribe concludes, "The Lord had humbled Judah because of Ahaz, for he had promoted wickedness in Judah and had been most unfaithful to the Lord " He lived wrongly and led poorly. Ultimately, the people did not respect Ahaz. At his death, the people did not bury him in the royal tombs.

Application - Chapter 8 - Jotham and Ahaz - Get Back In

It was a beautiful morning on the northeast Florida coast, so my young family and I decided to take a quick thirty-minute drive to the beach. My two young sons, ages six and five, were excited to spend some time in the refreshing shallow surf while my wife and I prepared to do some relaxing while feeding the marine life (otherwise known as fishing!). Our destination was a beautiful beach made up of many years of broken and collected coquina shells, a beach allowing cars to drive close to the breaking waves.

No sooner had we arrived at our spot until my two sons bolted out of the car and ran to the water's edge to splash and frolic in the less-than-foot-deep incoming tide. Before I even had time to remove our fishing gear from the car, our youngest son, Stephen, came screaming back to the car. He was holding his right hand with the left and letting out blood-curdling yells of "Something bit me, something bit me, something bit me!" My initial reaction was to think he had plopped down on a broken shell in the water and, having been much too familiar with *Jaws*, imagined a sharp bite of massive proportions. However, as he got closer to the car, we realized blood was profusely flowing from his hand and, upon applying pressure with a towel, we discovered a half-moon shape of small teeth marks running from his palm to the top of his hand. Something had bitten him!

Fortunately, we were only a few miles from Florida's Marineland, where those working in the area of marine biology could give us a quick assessment of the situation. After taking pictures and measurements of the bite's circumference, they informed us (with a fair degree of non-committal) that most likely Stephen had placed his hand on a semi-buried sand shark and received a "courtesy" bite from the creature to warn the boy not to move closer. "Whatever administered this bite," they said, "you can rest assured it could have been a lot worse, and you need to be thankful." We were!

The reason I bring this story up here is because of what happened next. I loaded a very fearful son back into the car and proceeded to take him back to the same spot on the beach we had just left. Doing what every "cruel father" would have done, I then took this screaming five-year-old and placed him back in the water where he had just been injured and traumatized! The reason? I knew if he did not get back in immediately, he would fear the water for the rest of his life and miss out on many beautiful times at the beach and in the surf as a result. To this day, over three decades later, he still loves the ocean!

It was because we made him "get back in!"

This chapter hopes to encourage those who have been "bitten" in the context of leadership life (this would be everyone!) but have been hesitant to move back into the arena or conviction that causes the wound (this would be too many!). May the words below serve as an impetus to help some "get back in" to that place of your divinely designed influence!

Courage – A Learned Behavior

Jotham exemplified courage founded on his confidence in God. However, Ahaz had seen his father's resolve in the face of significant threats and adversarial challenges and failed to exercise similar courage. When attacked, he ran to what appeared to be a visible source of strength that could be immediately accessed and was apparently quite successful. Though a natural response from Ahaz, this was, in essence, an act of cowardice and lack of trust in Yahweh. This father-and-son picture provides an understanding of courage in leadership that is very valuable and applicable for all. Courage was not, and is not, inherited as an innate characteristic through bloodlines or organizational structures. Neither does it automatically result from a positive model observed. Courage is a learned behavior developed daily.

While strong leaders have always been a vital part of societal structure and striving, the challenging and unprecedented transition, uncertainty, and upheaval the world is now experiencing make courageous leadership an invaluable and critical commodity. The need for strong leadership is especially relevant as the moral and ethical foundations of society are continually assaulted and challenged in the name of tolerance and a perverted understanding of love and unity.

Leaders would do well to relearn the exhilaration of standing firm in the face of adversity and attack to provide examples of fortitude for others to follow. The late world-renown evangelist Billy Graham expressed concern years ago when stating, "I feel sorry for the man who has never known the bracing thrill of taking a stand and sticking to it fearlessly. Moral courage has rewards that timidity can never imagine. Like a shot of adrenaline, it floods the Spirit with vitality... courage is contagious! When a brave man takes a stand, the spines of others are often stiffened."[52] If this was true in the turbulent times of the mid-1960s when Dr. Graham spoke these words, how much more is the admonition relevant for leaders navigating the concerns of 2021 and beyond!

The excellent news is the courage to lead strong and well in the 21st century is available and attainable. Courage is not an innate characteristic only a few possess but is a learned behavior available to all who long for it! Courage is learned behavior with observable and recognizable actions.

Some Research Observations

A plethora of books, articles, blogs, etc., have emerged in recent years accentuating the importance and prevalence of courage in 21st-century life and leadership. A quick inquiry via Google search shows over 280,000,000 areas of access available. Among these many conversations are studies from various disciplines and professional contexts that shed significant light on courage's nature. Four samples of these are referenced below in considerable detail. These samples should serve well to emphasize that courage is identifiable by specific practices and thus learned as a leadership competency.

Courage: A Skill[53]

Yet, in my 25 years of studying human behavior in organizations, I've discovered that courage in business seldom operates like this. Through interviews with more than 200 senior and mid-level managers who have acted courageously—whether on behalf of society, their companies, their colleagues, or their careers—I've learned that this kind of courage is rarely impulsive. Nor does it emerge from nowhere.

In business, courageous action is a special kind of calculated risk-taking. People who become good leaders have a greater than average willingness to make bold moves. They strengthen their chances of success—and avoid career suicide—through careful deliberation and preparation. Business courage is not a visionary leader's inborn characteristic as a skill acquired through decision-making processes that improve with practice. In other words, most great business leaders teach themselves to make high-risk decisions. They learn to do this well over a period of time, often decades.

Courage: Cultivated daily[54]

I began investigating workplace courage after spending more than a decade studying why people so often don't speak up at work. I've found many examples of people at all levels who created positive change without ruining their careers. Their success rested primarily on a learned set of attitudes and behaviors rather than on innate characteristics. I call people who exhibit these behaviors *competently courageous* because they create the right conditions for action by establishing a strong internal reputation and improving their fallback options if things go poorly. They carefully choose their battles, discerning whether a given opportunity to act makes sense in light of their values, the timing, and broader objectives; they maximize the odds of in-the-moment success by managing the messaging and emotions, and they follow up to preserve relationships and marshal commitment. These steps are useful whether you're pushing for significant change or trying to address a smaller or more local issue. Lest anyone think I'm naive, let me be clear: Of course, bad things do happen when people challenge authorities, norms, and institutions. Courage, after all, is about taking worthy actions *despite the potential risk.*

Courage: Six attributes[55]

- **Feeling fear yet choosing to act** (do it anyway!)

"I learned that courage was not the absence of fear, but the triumph over it. The brave man is not he who does not feel afraid, but he who conquers that fear." —*Nelson Mandela*

"Courage is about doing what you're afraid to do. There can be no courage unless you're scared. Have the courage to act instead of react." —*Oliver Wendell Holmes*

- **Following your heart** (power of passion)

"To dare is to lose one's footing momentarily. To not dare is to lose oneself." —*Soren Kierkegaard*

"Passion is what drives us crazy, what makes us do extraordinary things, to discover, to challenge ourselves.

Passion is and should always be the heart of courage." —
Midori Komatsu

- **Persevering in the face of adversity** (no such thing as "smooth sailing")

"A hero is no braver than an ordinary man, but he is braver five minutes longer." —*Ralph Waldo Emerson*

"It's not the size of the dog in the fight, it's the size of the fight in the dog." —*Mark Twain*

- **Standing up for what is right** (conviction)

"Sometimes standing against evil is more important than defeating it. The greatest heroes stand because it is right to do so, not because they believe they will walk away with their lives. Such selfless courage is a victory in itself." —*N.D. Wilson*

"Anger is the prelude to courage." —*Eric Hoffer*

- **Expanding your horizons; Letting go of the familiar** (comfort becomes uncomfortable)

"Man cannot discover new oceans unless he has the courage to lose sight of the shore." —*Lord Chesterfield*

"This world demands the qualities of youth; not a time of life but a state of mind, a temper of the will, a quality of the imagination, a predominance of courage over timidity, of the appetite for adventure over the life of ease." —*Robert F. Kennedy*

- **Facing suffering with dignity or faith** (avoidance of difficulty is not top priority)

"There is no need to be ashamed of tears, for tears bear witness that a man has the greatest of courage, the courage to suffer." —*Viktor Frankl*

"The ideal man bears the accidents of life with dignity and grace, making the best of circumstances." —*Aristotle*

Courage at work: Brené Brown[56]

Daring leadership. As part of her research, Brené asked hundreds of leaders which skills would be most important for leaders of the future. The one answer that emerged from the data was courage. What do courageous and brave leaders look like? Based on her research, this is what brave leaders do each day:

Have difficult conversations: Courageous leaders have the challenging, sometimes emotional conversations, even when they don't want to.

Embrace fears and feelings: Courageous leaders understand they need to spend time attending to the fears and feelings of their employees or spend a significant amount of time dealing with the impact of these feelings and fears. These leaders understand that they need to embrace what is driving (workplace) fears…

Show people how to re-set: Courageous leaders encourage people to make mistakes, reset, and bounce back. In fact, these leaders would rather hire someone who is not perfect but has the ability to bounce back and learn from mistakes.

Focus on the root cause: Courageous leaders focus on problem-solving and getting to the root cause of issues. Although it's easy to find a quick fix, a courageous leader stays in the problem to determine the cause. Once the cause is found, they go into problem-solving mode.

Have the conversations around diversity and inclusion: Courageous leaders are never quiet about discussing the hard topics around diversity and inclusion. To not want to have these difficult conversations is the definition of privilege. Brave leaders choose courage over comfort. It is not the job of the people targeted by racism to invite people to the conversation. It is the role of the leader to start the conversation.

Do not shame or blame: Courageous leaders do not shame and blame others. They understand that when you humiliate someone, that person will quickly become disengaged. Shaming and blaming come from a place of control, not a place of vulnerability.

Brené's research revealed 4 key skills required to be a courageous leader…each of these can be learned:

Skill #1: Rumbling with vulnerability: Courageous leaders embrace their vulnerability, even when it's uncomfortable. Many of us were raised to believe that vulnerability is a weakness and at the same time, that we needed to be brave. The reality is you cannot have courage and bravery without vulnerability. Many leaders are afraid to let the "gooey" center of emotions be on display at work. The challenge is this "gooey" center (as Brené calls it) is the same place where love, belonging, and joy originate. Data tells us that belonging is one of the key facets that drive engagement, productivity, and retention in an organization. Belonging is about employees bringing their whole selves to work and speaking their truth. A culture of belonging is one where it's safe to experiment when innovating. It is only through expressing vulnerability that a culture of belonging emerges.

Skill #2: Living your values: When organizations state their core values but do not operationalize these values, all that is left is "bull****," says Brené. People will make up what the values mean and then use the values to justify behavior. Courageous leaders operationalize values into specific behaviors.

Skill #3: Braving trust: "Clear is kind. Unclear is unkind," says Brené. Courageous leaders need to be clear with their teams on what is working and what is not. Employees need to understand where they stand on projects, development, and growth. To give this clarity to employees is both kind and difficult. It requires challenging and honest conversations. Leaders need to learn they can be tough and tender; fierce and kind; and drive hard change while also recognizing people. It takes bravery, and it takes practice.

Skill #4: Learning to rise: A courageous leaders (sic) recognize when their head starts to make up stories at work. They realize these stories are based on assumptions and fear. Courageous leaders understand that the stories they make up can create challenging work situations. These leaders use self-reflection to recognize that the stories are just that, stories. They can then start look at facts and lead from knowledge versus fear and incorrect stories. Courageous leaders cultivate a culture in which brave work, tough conversations, and whole hearts are the norm. Courageous leaders understand that "heart matters" at work.[56]

From the examples above and reflections on many other conversations on the topic of courage, a working definition/description with very practical, behavioral applications is in order: Courage is the predetermined commitment to do the right thing regardless of ramifications and personal costs that may result.[57] From this definition, one can easily recognize three crucial considerations that characterize courageous living and leadership: a predetermined commitment, a sense of "right," and the realization of a potential cost involved.[58]

Courage – A Divine Command

One of the most outstanding biblical illustrations of the necessity of courage during times of transition times is Joshua's leadership, Moses's successor. Joshua's call was to "fill some big shoes" and, in doing so, lead Israel into the long-awaited entrance and conquering of the Promised Land.

As the book of Joshua opens, Moses is dead, and this assistant-turned-successor is certainly apprehensive and somewhat afraid. A quick self-assessment brought questions and concerns as he receives the Divine commission to be strong, courageous, and clear-headed as he plans the invasion of the land on the "other side of Jordan" (Josh. 1:1-9)! F. B. Meyer artfully describes below what must have been going on in the heart and mind of Joshua as this transition with new responsibilities lingered over him:

> As Joshua stood on the threshold of his great work, he was repeatedly bidden to be strong and of a good courage. Some little time before the death of his predecessor, a great convocation of all Israel had been summoned, at which Moses solemnly transferred his office to his successor and had given him the charge, saying, 'Be strong and of a good courage; for thou must go with this people unto the land.' And now the voice of God reiterates the charge and repeats the injunction…Probably he had never dreamt of so high an honor, so vast a responsibility…When therefore the call came to him to assume the office which Moses was vacating, his heart failed him, and he needed every kind of encouragement and stimulus, both from God and man…Joshua's task was a very difficult one…The Jewish legend says that when Joshua, appalled at the greatness of the task, rent his clothes and fell on his face, weeping the think of his incompetence. Moses lifted him up and comforted him with the assurance that God had foreseen and provided for all.[59]

Perhaps the foreboding nature of this transition necessitated a COMMAND from both Moses and thrice by God (Deut. 31:7; Josh. 1:6-9) as related to the courage required for the occasion? This was no mere suggestion or wishful thinking but an absolute imperative if the mission ahead were to see accomplishment! Much was at stake.

A Resourced Command

One thing is for sure: God will not command something of His people and those leading others that He will not make provision to accomplish. He does not set people up for failure and assignments of frustration and futility. When Joshua receives the command to be strong, it was possible to do so, regardless of the apparent obstacles ahead in the process of taking the land promised to Israel. As has been popularly proclaimed, "He makes provision for the vision." Part of that provision is the ability to develop courage as needed!

There is little doubt that leadership in the 21st century, especially post-2020, is fraught with difficulties and unprecedented challenges. It is also without question that courage is an essential aspect of a leader's competency kit to realize a God-designed sense of success. The command to be courageous still sends out a clarion call in the present contexts of churches, businesses, non-profits, corporations, etc. (anywhere there are Christ-centered leaders!) as distinctly and urgently as heard by the son of Nun on the eastern banks of Jordan many years ago. The same resources to develop courage are available as well!

Joshua took advantage of two primary resources that allowed him to prosper in developing courage and the corresponding pursuit of the promises awaiting in Canaan. First, God's promised presence accompanied the leader and people as they move forward to conquer the land (Josh. 1:9). It would be the ever-abiding presence of the "senior partner" in this endeavor that served to bring strength, courage, direction, and protection to Joshua and Israel when fighting enemies more powerful than them. Second, a constant emersion into the "law of the Lord" is a prerequisite to prosperity in the plan and process (Josh. 1:7-8). Joshua's mind and heart were to be formed by the word of God and parameters of both thought and behavior established by its instruction.

Leaders in the 21st century would do well to give heed to these empowering resources as "new territory" lies ahead!

A Repeated Command

It is interesting to note that God and Joshua's predecessor, Moses, did not only expect courage, but this was also repeated and required by the people. The nation gathered to Joshua to express their support of his leadership and commitment to the vision and work ahead (Josh. 1:16-18). However, the one requirement expressed from them was for the new leader to "only be strong and of good courage" (1:18b).

In days of extreme upheaval and uncertainty, there are just things that are non-negotiable in people's minds asked to take the journey into uncharted territory. Topping the list of these deal-breakers is the necessity of courage in leadership. People do not expect perfection or even absolute certainty regarding every decision made. Still, they demand leaders to be courageous enough to stand behind decisions and follow-through when opposition arises. This principle is observed often with Joshua as the Canaanites did not give up their land without intense fighting. It must also be true for leaders in 21st-century contexts facing great opportunities but unprecedented challenges.

A Reciprocal Command

A final observation in this brief overview of courage and Joshua's call to leadership is related to the leader's expectation from the people. While God, Moses, and the people expected Joshua to be very strong and courageous, Joshua outlines this same commitment required from the people (Josh. 10:25; 23:6-7). Courage among leaders and those following is a reciprocal arrangement!

Moving any organization forward into new territory is never a spectator sport where most constituents sit in the stands and watch the "professionals" play. The spectator syndrome proves to yield many "armchair quarterbacks" who, while sipping on Dr. Pepper and eating hot dogs, second-guess, criticize decisions, and demand better performance from those actually in the game. This practice is always counter-productive. However, when spectators are required to become courageous participants in decision-making and actual implementation, things drastically change! Joshua was not fighting the battles for Israel but leading Israel into conflicts that would benefit the entire nation but demanded the courage and commitment of all.

Joshua knew leaders could only expect what they are willing to model. Modeling courage allowed him the social equity to require it of others.

A Final Word

As the story of the shark bite opened this discussion on courage, this chapter, while applicable to all leaders in any context, is specifically designed to encourage some who have left their leadership dreams (and calling!) and somehow settled into the status quo, the path of least resistance. Because of "bites" received along the way, the courage that once characterized one's leadership and vocational calling is now a distant memory.

Now is the time to reengage and "get back in!" Yes, the sharks are still there and getting bitten in both a possibility and probability. But receiving the courage of Jotham and resisting the cowardice of Ahaz will bring great fruit!

Chapter Nine – King Hezekiah - (728-686) 2 Kings 18-20; 2 Chronicles 29-32

Both the narratives in 2 Kings and 2 Chronicles, devote a larger section to the esteemed leader King Hezekiah than to most of the kings. The accounts acclaim him as, "No king of Judah, among either his predecessors or his successors, could be compared to him." In 2015 the Israeli archaeologist, Eilat Mazar, discovered a royal seal of Hezekiah.[60] The bullah reads, "Belonging to Hezekiah, son of Ahaz king of Judah." The date of the seal's origin ranges from 727–698 B.C., the same timeframe for Hezekiah. We can broadly divide his reign into three major actions.

1. Restoring of the Faith

King Hezekiah enacted sweeping religious reforms. His mother, Abijah (also called Abi), was a daughter of the high priest Zechariah. The strong influence of his godly mother appears to affect Hezekiah positively. He had the priests go through the temple and remove any pagan items that his father Ahaz had installed. The items must have been many, for it took the priests 16 days to accomplish the task.

Hezekiah went through the land of Judah thoroughly demolishing false idols. He had the priests sanctify the priesthood, temple, festivals, and a host of other items. A great Passover celebration was held in Jerusalem with invitations sent throughout the region of Israel and Judah. The Passover event was a great success. The revival inspired even the visiting northern Israelites to return home and remove their idols.

2. Resisting the Assyrians

In Hezekiah's day, the northern kingdom of Israel fell to the Assyrians in 722 B.C. The aggression of the Assyrians would not stop in the north. Hezekiah knew these realities. Near this timeframe, Sargon II mentions Hezekiah in his inscriptions.[61] Hezekiah diligently prepared his nation for the worst. A major water tunnel of more than 1,500 feet was dug to supply the city of Jerusalem in case of a siege.[62] He enlarged and strengthened walls. He made a preemptive gain into the Philistine area.

The day came when Sargon II's son, Sennacherib, invaded Judah. He devastated many cities and took many hostages. Hezekiah gave some tribute money to Sennacherib, hoping to end the carnage. Sennacherib accepted the tribute but continued to oppress Jerusalem as well. Sennacherib devoted more than 60 feet of wall space in his palace to his campaign with Hezekiah.[63]

In the chaos of this national crisis, the prophet Isaiah prophesied that "God would deal with Sennacherib. Jerusalem will not fall. He will return home and eventually die in the temple of his god." Indeed, Sennacherib's army mysteriously died by the thousands. Herodotus recorded that mice came into the camp, adding that the Egyptians later erected a monument to Sennacherib's humiliation.[64] Assyrian records confirm that Sennacherib's sons murdered him while he was worshipping in the temple of his god, Nisroch.[65]

3. Repenting of His Pride

At some point, Hezekiah fell deathly ill. When he was at the point of death, the text informs us that he greatly humbled himself. Amazingly, he recovered from his illness and lived another 15 years as the prophet Isaiah predicted. Eliat Mazar's team discovered a seal with the name of Isaiah and possibly the word "prophet" on it only 10 feet from where they discovered the Hezekiah seal.[66]

Sometime after his improvement, Hezekiah received congratulatory letters on his recovery from Baladan, king of Babylon. Hezekiah received the envoys and pridefully revealed all his treasure, spices, oil, and armory among his treasuries. Isaiah later corrected the king about his pride. Isaiah prophesied correctly that one day all the treasure that Hezekiah bragged about will be taken to Babylon, along with many captives.

Conclusion on King Hezekiah

On the positive side, many marvelous points can be repeated about King Hezekiah. He set the nation in order spiritually and militarily. He went above and beyond what anyone could expect of an exceptionally good king. The one criticism raised at the end concerned his pride. While the actual chronology of this event most likely preceded that of the Sennacherib invasion years earlier, the scribe chose to place it at the end of the biography on Hezekiah. Why? The reason may lie in covering all the many positives about Hezekiah but ending with the danger of pride for all of us. Certainly, the topic of pride leads well into the next chapter on his arrogant son, Manasseh.

Application - Chapter Nine - Hezekiah - Resourced from Within

Living in Florida, it is not uncommon but never comfortable in late spring and early summer to see trees, plants, grass, and even wildlife begin to droop and start to wither from the lack of moisture. Finally, just in the nick of time, it seems, life-restoring drops of vitality will fall from the sky to saturate a thirsty landscape. It was delightful last night to hear the thunder introducing that much-needed downpour of rain.

My wife and I enjoyed this morning the immediate visual effects of the storm experienced last evening. Enriching our usual "coffee and conversation" time were comments about the refreshing in the air, diamond-drops of moisture reflecting the rays of the rising sun, and the overnight change of color and renewed strength evident in the surrounding landscape. You see, we attempt to sustain our property through periodic watering and maintenance, but the remarkable difference one significant rain makes causes our feeble attempt to keep things alive to pale in comparison. As I soaked in the greening, blooming, and fruit-producing results of the shower, I considered afresh what a difference we would experience in our lives if we could just see a "good rain."

Too often, our personal lives and even our churches are leaning heavily upon humanly devised methods in an attempt to "irrigate" the apparent dryness and all-too-close-to-dying environment. Just like my landscaping, these sprinkles may help keep death at bay for a while, but this ultimately bears little resemblance to the vibrant life that a real deluge from heaven could accomplish!

However, as useful as the sources of irrigation and rainfall are, they are dependent on external factors (piping, seasons, etc.) that can fall far short of providing the amount of water needed. Fortunate indeed is the one who can locate a vital source of water that flows underground, is not dependent on external conditions, and from which roots of thirsty trees and plants nearby can tap into and draw from in abundance. This picture is painted in Psalm 1 when the author expresses the blessing of being a "tree planted by rivers of water" whose vitality is continuous and fruit-bearing is consistent! From ancient times, the construction of whole civilizations and the individual units that constitute those have begun with the discovery of deep-water sources to sustain survival and allow for expansion and prosperity.

Water is life and accessing a continual supply of the life-giving flow is essential!

From the Inside Out: Hezekiah's Renovation

The historical backdrop of the potential conflict between Judah and Assyria is critical in appreciating some of King Hezekiah's acts.

One of his most memorable and celebrated acts involved the rerouting of Jerusalem's water supply in anticipation of an Assyrian army's eventual siege. Hezekiah recognized Judah's capital city's vulnerability with its primary source of water located outside the city wall. Somehow, to give the city (and nation) a chance to survive an attack and city siege, the water must be channeled inside the walls so that this life-supply would flow from the inside-out rather than having to be brought from the outside-in. Leaving the city's water supply at the disposal of an attacking enemy meant immediate surrender or a relatively swift, water-deprived death.

The plan resulted in the digging of an underground aqueduct system that rerouted the water supply from the Gihon Springs outside the Jerusalem city walls to a reservoir dug inside the city (Pool of Siloam).

> Hezekiah's Tunnel, part of Jerusalem's water system, is located under the City of David. It connects the Gihon Spring—Jerusalem's freshwater supply—with the Siloam Pool. According to 2 Chronicles 32:2–4 and 2 Kings 20:20, during the reign of King Hezekiah of Judah, the execution of this tunnel digging prepared Jerusalem for the Assyrian king's (Sennacherib) imminent attack Sennacherib. In the Bible, Hezekiah redirected the water through old and newly dug Jerusalem tunnels.[67]

While there has been some discussion in recent years over the dating and actual route of the tunnel dug, there is little doubt that King Hezekiah's wisdom and execution of this plan was both an engineering marvel and had the potential of assisting the residents of Jerusalem in resisting the onslaught of the Assyrian invaders. Maeir and Chadwick further explain this in light of Hezekiah's overall strategy against the encroaching enemy:

> That the revolt of Hezekiah began in 705 B.C.E., directly after the death in battle of Sargon II, king of Assyria, is an accepted historical fact. Similar revolts by other Assyrian vassals in other parts of the empire occurred at the same time. Sargon's successor, Sennacherib, was occupied quelling the revolts in the east during the first three years after Sargon's death. It was only four years after Sennacherib's coronation in 701 B.C.E. that he was able to turn west and conduct his ferocious campaign against Judah.

In the four years between the commencement of Hezekiah's revolt and the arrival of Sennacherib in Judah, Hezekiah made ready for the inevitable Assyrian response. He put together a coalition of western kings to form a united front against Assyria (this alliance quickly fell apart when the Assyrians actually arrived in the Levant). In addition, he made all kinds of material preparations at home in Judah (see 2 Chronicles 32:2–8), including fortifying Jerusalem and various towns in the kingdom, preparing weapons, storing food and supplies (for which LMLK storage jars were probably utilized) and, of course, improving Jerusalem's water system (2 Chronicles 32:30). Most scholars accept that the Siloam Tunnel ("Hezekiah's Tunnel") was part of this effort.[68]

This 1750 feet of underground channel, discovered by Edward Robinson in 1838, is still a prominent site in the City of David (just south of the Temple Mount in Jerusalem). Many tourists visit this attraction each year to navigate the quarter mile-plus tunnel confines through walls that average a height of less than six feet, a width of 23-26 inches, and water depth from almost dry to chest high (depending on rainfall). It has been a joy to lead many students and church groups through the tunnel and actually watch grown men emerge from the journey with both sighs of relief and shouts of triumph!

To bring it home, what translated into the Judeans' potential survival was the importance of having a source of water that flowed from the inside-out, not the outside-in! SURVIVING AND THRIVING AS A CHRIST-CENTERED LEADER IN THE 21st CENTURY REQUIRES NO LESS!

From the Inside-out: Jesus' Proclamation

Being "resourced from within" was the obvious point of Jesus' famous outcry during the final day of the eight-day Feast of Tabernacles. This feast included various ceremonies focusing on God's goodness in supplying water (often supernaturally) for the Israelites during their history. The "water" emphasis was understandable in that the nation's survival amidst desert conditions was always in the forefront as both a source of celebration and ongoing concern. Now taking the "waterworks" metaphor to a new level, Jesus exclaims during this celebration, "Let anyone who is thirsty come to me and drink. Whoever believes in me, as Scripture has said, rivers of living water will flow from within them" (John 7:37-38, NIV).

John explains the true meaning of this when instructing the reader that this was speaking of the infilling and overflowing of the Holy Spirit who was yet to be given (7:39). It is important to note that this is not a source of life that would come upon them from an external source, but instead will "flow from within them!" Resourced from within is the promise from Jesus of empowerment that is not controlled or even manipulated by external circumstances! Just as Hezekiah would not leave the well-being of Jerusalem to an external water supply that the Assyrians could destroy, Jesus would not leave his people and the leaders among them to the uncertainties of cultural change, threats of demonic attack, or difficulties from natural occurrences. Being resourced from within allows for the very practical application of the realization that "greater is he that is *in you* than he that is in the world" (1 John 4:4b, italics mine).

From the Inside-out: Jesus' Command

Men and women are waiting in Jerusalem for the fulfillment of a promise (Acts 1). A seemingly impossible commission tasks these people with taking the message of the Kingdom of God to a world characterized by religious pluralism, harsh political dominance, and moral decadence. No doubt, there was much excitement in the air as they had actually received these instructions from the resurrected Jesus! There was no doubt that there was much intrinsic motivation connected to this excitement as they desired to be an active part of the Kingdom expansion proposed by the King Himself! However, the strange thing is that even though commissioned, excited, and motivated, the king knew his messengers would face obstacles and challenges far beyond the capacities of temporary excitement and fluctuating motivation to overcome. The mission was clear, but power for the purpose was yet to come. Jesus commanded them to wait for proper equipment before setting out on the adventure, knowing that even a well-defined mission without sufficient empowerment becomes "mission impossible."

While studying Acts 1 recently, it became apparent how much "church stuff" can occur without the promised Pentecostal empowerment insisted upon by Jesus. BEFORE the outpouring of the promised Holy Spirit in Acts 2, the disciples were very busy doing good "church" stuff. They were: 1) anticipating the second coming of Jesus (1:11), 2) exercising obedience (1:12), 3) assembling for prayer (1:13-14a), 4) gathering together in unity (1:14a), 5) creating a culture of diversity and equality (1:14b), 6) conducting business (1:15-22), 7) reflecting on the scriptures (1:16,20), 7) electing/appointing leaders (1:21-26), 8) and recognizing the centrality of the resurrection (1:22b). It is truly remarkable to realize all of these things were taking place before the pouring out on these people of the promise of power for the proposed purpose! Could we even fathom this group looking around at all the systems in place and saying, "We're doing pretty well as is; maybe waiting and dependence on the promise of the Spirit is not that big of a deal?"

Fast-forward now to a time more than two thousand years beyond Acts 1 and the disciples-in-waiting. We perceive a similar call of mammoth proportions but also seemingly insurmountable odds. The 21st-century church and its leaders become heirs of the commission to reach their world with the transformational gospel of the Risen Christ. This task also to be done in the midst of rampant relativism, constant social and political unrest, unnerving economic downturns and vocational uncertainties, extreme dangers from organized terrorist groups and "lone wolf" murderers, unending attacks on the Christian faith, world-wide pandemics, and many other manifestations of latter-time, "perilous" surroundings (2 Timothy 3:1-5).

Could it be that the same solution given to the first-century church is also the God-ordained answer for provision needed for the 21st century?

Could it be the tasks of "making disciples of all people" (Matthew 28:19-20), becoming "salt and light" amid darkness and decay (Matthew 5:13-14), and in leading a prepared people into Kingdom service (Ephesians 4:11-12) is hanging on desperation for and pursuit of being "resourced from within?"

Could it be that an overdependence on human expertise, trends of excitement, and cleverly devised motivational tactics are hindering the realization of God's "inside-out" solution?

Could it be that the proliferation of humanism of recent decades has so infiltrated the church that we find ourselves succumbing to the tendency to trust in our abilities, education, talent, models, and experience MORE THAN an ongoing infilling of the Holy Spirit (Ephesians 5:18)?

Suppose the answer to any of these is a resounding YES. In that case, we must vigorously resist this rip current of compromise, dragging us into deeper depths of ineffectiveness while eternally lost, hurting people in need of Christ are perishing without ever knowing His love!

From the Inside-out: Three Considerations

When one realizes the critical importance of any Christ-follower and Christ-centered leader being "resourced from within," three considerations may help in self-evaluating whether or not the "underground water source" is genuinely functioning in our lives.

First, preachers and teachers should realistically evaluate message emphases and salient points to assess how much they are encouraging constituents to seek initial and continual infillings of the Holy Spirit. In other words, is the importance of the infilling and overflowing of the Holy Spirit simply an espoused value with little real-life application, or is this a real value presented as essential equipment for the effective believer and church leader? Am I leading those within my influence to "be being filled with the Spirit" (see Ephesians 5:18) as a matter of daily priority?

Second, individuals should honestly evaluate how many of their life-decisions are made under the invited supervision of the Spirit rather than through trial-and-error, personal preference, or the advice of others. While these three "alternatives" are not essentially wrong, are my decisions reflecting a true Spirit-dependence? Are other means of decision-making always subservient to His influence and direction? Those resourced from within do not seek the Spirit's guidance as a last resort but perceive His counsel as a prioritized possibility in every situation!

Finally, being resourced from within with power for purpose not only refers to mission and task but is first manifested in the lifestyle and attitude. Developing fruit along with gifts is essential for message validation and authentic influence! A person resourced from within understands the futility of charisma without character, position without spiritual passion, and personality without power! Is my relationship with Jesus more important in my self-identity than a position of influence in an organizational context (even the church)? Is my lifegoal to become continually conformed to the image of Christ (Romans 8:29) and daily model His life and holiness to those around me?

While self-assessment efforts can tend to be uncomfortable, it is in this very discomfort that healing and rejuvenation can take place. May it be so on all of us as we honestly look at these and other questions about our real source of strength and effectiveness!

A Final Thought

As I write this chapter's final words, I am sitting at my desk looking outside at yet another beautiful rainy evening. The rain is especially beautiful this evening because just yesterday, I transplanted some large plants from their pots into the ground in my backyard. When planting them, I looked at my wife and said these words, "Now they need some water."

From an ancient king who saw the need for water from within, not without, to a Savior who promised water that flows from our "innermost being," may we also long for that place where living waters flow and will bring "resource from within!"

Chapter Ten – King Manasseh and King Amon – (697-640) 2 Kings 21; 2 Chronicles 33

In this chapter we have combined the father and son kings of Manasseh and Amon. Manasseh had the longest reign of any of the Judean kings. Ironically, his son Amon had one of the shortest reigns of a mere two years. Naturally, Amon's narrative is noticeably short in the biblical text. Our examination of Manasseh will serve as the main section of this important time period. We can view his reign in terms of three location periods in his life.

1. In Jerusalem as King

By embracing the abominations of the heathen nations, Manasseh quickly sought to reverse the positive reforms instituted by his godly father, Hezekiah. He took a keen interest in worshipping the astrological hosts. An article published in 1963 covered an interesting seal with the inscription "Manasseh son of the king." [69] We cannot be positive the seal is Manasseh's, but the seal fits his timeframe. Also, the picture graph contains the pagan worship symbols of a star and crescent. Hebrew seals rarely contained these images.

Manasseh had a strong fascination with satanic practices manifested through mediums, omens, sorcery, and witchcraft. He sacrificed his own children in the fire to false gods. He even erected a graven image in the temple along with altars to other gods. Because of his actions, Jerusalem was filled with the deaths of innocent people. The prophets were among this group of innocent people killed, as they were put to the sword (Jer. 2:30). The prophet Jeremiah further adds that the Babylonian exile was due in large part to Manasseh's evil reign (Jer. 15:4). The royal record sums this section up with, "Manasseh made Judah worse than the surrounding heathen nations."

2. In Babylon as Prisoner

The prophets admonished Manasseh, but to no avail. He refused to listen. Therefore, "The Lord allowed the army commanders of the king of Assyria to take Manasseh prisoner, put a hook in his nose, bound him with bronze shackles and [took] him to Babylon." In his great distress, Manasseh repented of his sin, and God had mercy on him. Eventually, the Assyrian king, who is not named, allows Manasseh to return back to Judah and reassume his regal duties as king.

Two Assyrian kings mentioned Manasseh in their inscriptions. Esarhaddon lists Manasseh in a coalition of 22 kings required to assist in a major construction project that he described as occurring "under terrible conditions."[70] After Esarhaddon's death, his son Ashurbanipal also listed Manasseh in a coalition of kings that were required to contribute to his invasion force against Egypt.[71] Manasseh may have named his son Amon after the Egyptian city No-Amon (Thebes), that he helped Ashurbanipal to conquer near 663 B.C. (Nahum 3:8; Jer. 46:25; Eze. 30:15-16).[72]

Ashurbanipal appeared to be the best candidate for Manasseh's imprisonment. First, Ashurbanipal had already experimented with the method of imprisoning Pharaoh Necho I, deporting him and others as prisoners to Nineveh.[73] In time, Ashurbanipal pardoned Necho and reinstated him as pharaoh, along with his possessions and territories, and even gave him new ones. In the Necho's case, the pardoning worked. The twenty-sixth dynasty of Egypt began with Necho I and remained pro-Assyria for many years. Ashurbanipal's inscription connects Manasseh with his Egyptian campaign, which may have sparked his gamble on releasing another prisoner king.

Second, the biblical text states that Manasseh was captured and sent to Babylon. In 652–648, Ashurbanipal had the unpleasant task of culling a Babylonian revolt headed by his own brother.[74] A number of subjugated nations also participated in the rebellion. Manasseh may have participated. The text mentions Manasseh later repairing damaged walls which may have resulted from a revolt.

Eventually, Babylon was retaken, and Ashurbanipal's brother committed suicide by burning the palace down upon himself. Additionally, the rebelling kings were also punished. Babylon would have been a fitting place to bring the imprisoned kings. They would be able to see the burned palace of the rebellious king they so foolishly chose to support.

Third, the most likely timing of Manasseh's imprisonment was in his final years as king. The Babylonian revolt in 652–648 fits into Manasseh's last few years of leadership. When he returned to Jerusalem, he sought to make amends for the harm his wayward leadership had made on Judah. In spite of his best efforts, he could not totally bring the nation back from idolatry. Even his son, Amon, quickly returned to idolatry practices once he was installed as king. Such a narrative logically points to a short restoration period by Manasseh that did not allow him to enact long-lasting reforms.

3. Back in Jerusalem as King

The repentance of Manasseh was genuine. Upon his return to Jerusalem, he set about making things right. A king's first responsibility involved the people's physical defense; therefore, he rebuilt and reinforced the cities in Judah. As to the nation's spiritual defenses, he removed the foreign gods, the idolatrous image in the temple, false altars, and restored proper worship guidelines.

Conclusion on King Manasseh and King Amon

Whereas some of the Judean kings began well but did not end well, Manasseh's case is the opposite. He ended well in spite of a horrendous beginning. This proves that none are beyond help. The harsh reality of prison awakened the king to the spiritual prison into which he had locked his nation. The account of his reign was preserved in the records of the prophets — the very group he once opposed and persecuted. Thankfully, they could positively write at the end of his life, "Then Manasseh knew that the Lord is God."

Application - Chapter 10 - Manasseh (and Amon) - With Eternity in Mind

It was a beautiful day on the Gulf coast as my family and I enjoyed our annual vacation together. The sun was shining, waves rolled in gently, and people were taking advantage of the serene surroundings in a variety of ways. It was later in the afternoon that my wife came up with a plan.

Being the creative artist, she suggested that six of us (including two smaller grandchildren) begin constructing a sand sculpture that would be "life-size" and as realistic as possible with sand as the primary ingredient. Since I was absent the day they passed out artistic ability, my first response was a slight grimace but eventually transitioned to the willingness to cooperate as a "go-fer." You know... the one that contributes to the project by obeying the command to "go for" the next batch of supplies, etc. So, the work on the masterpiece began.

For about an hour and a half, the sand sculpture labor was quite intense but also rewarding as the shape of a large dolphin began to emerge out of the sand complete with fins, tail, snout, and an open mouth full of teeth, and even a real crab inserted into the mouth for good measure. It was amazing both to the many passersby who commented on the project and to us. Many even stopped to ask if they could take a picture with it! However, as the sun began to get closer to the horizon, it became apparent that this afternoon of fun, laughter, and creative expression was coming to an end.

Our condo room was on the fourth floor of the building, sitting right on the shore and having a balcony that allowed us to continue to observe our creation and the reactions of others that continued to pass by. I basked with great satisfaction in the view as people would pause and point at various features of the "dolphin," young hand-holding lovers would pose for a picture, and most everyone seemed to approach the masterpiece with a sense of awe. Until…

Out of the corner of my eye, I spied a couple with two young boys (probably 8-10 years old) who were walking our way and soon spotted the sculpture. From my lofty vantage point, I stood almost paralyzed as the boys launched into a full sprint toward the dolphin with obvious destructive intent accompanied by ever-increasing hilarity! As though a gold medal in the Olympic long jump was at stake, it was evident as the scene unfolded that the first one to plant their feet into the sculpted sand was the "winner!" While tempted to scream a loud and extended "no…….," I realized the distance and sound of the surf would make my attempt at verbal intervention powerless and futile. I could do nothing but watch as the boys gleefully smashed our masterpiece into unrecognizable form in a matter of a few seconds.

Rising early the next morning to have coffee on that same balcony, I looked toward the sculpture's location. While knowing the general area, the actual site or structure was no longer discernable. During the night, the incoming tide had thoroughly washed away any evidence of the masterpiece created the day before.

I reminded myself while standing and contemplating the scenario of how common it is to spend a lot of time and energy creating something in/with our lives that will be gone "in the morning." When the ebbs and flows of this life are gone and eternity has dawned, how much of what I have labored so hard for will still be standing? How much of my effort will yield lasting fruit and have an eternal impact?

Forgetting the Eternal

Manasseh is often called the most corrupt king of the southern kingdom of Judah. While the longest-reigning monarch of this area, his fifty-five years of power and influence took a significant negative toll on the nation, eventually culminating in their deportation into Babylonian captivity (Jer. 15:4). Additionally, as mentioned in the historical overview earlier in this chapter, Manasseh's son and successor ruled only two years. His father's policies and practices obviously impacted his short and wicked reign.

It is interesting to note that Manasseh's name has the connotation of "forgetting," as can be seen in an earlier Israelite of the same name, Joseph's first son (Gen. 41:51).[75] In Joseph's case, he named his firstborn in Egypt "Manasseh: cause to forget" to celebrate God's goodness in taking him through great difficulty and promoting him to great prominence. God's present blessings caused him to "forget" the hardships previously experienced. However, when looking at Manasseh, king of Judah, his name takes on a whole new and dark significance. This king seemed adamant about causing Judah to "forget" God's commands and correspondingly take on the prohibited practices of the heathen nations around them.

Corruption and a myriad of destructive actions result anytime a people forget to celebrate their calling and covenant with God. When the temporal becomes preeminent and the eternal forgotten, trouble and mayhem will abound and overtake good fruit more quickly than weeds in an unkempt summer garden. Forgetting the eternal will often be manifested by the growth of some of the following "weeds."

Forgetting the Eternal: Warnings Ignored

2 Chronicles 23 describes King Manasseh as one adamant about ignoring the past. God had delivered Israel from the pagan practices that this wicked king was bent on restoring (vs. 2). Not only did he ignore the revival and removal of idolatry carried out by his father Hezekiah (vs. 3), but activity expressly forbidden and condemned as far back as the reigns of David and Solomon was arrogantly re-instituted in the nation (vss. 4-8). Also, though prophets had been sent to the

king on various occasions to remind him of the backsliding climate he was creating and the fruit that would result, the idolatrous agenda at hand caused these warnings to be shoved aside as unimportant and irrelevant wrangling and roadblocks (2 Kings 21:10-15).

One of the most significant gifts people possess is the ability to observe, evaluate, and do course correction as needed. People are not slaves to ingrained instinct or learned behaviors like animals with only reactionary reflexes based on primary external stimuli. Leaders need to exercise an even greater propensity to learn valuable lessons from observing others' behaviors, good and bad. Manasseh appeared to be completely oblivious to the positive effects of his father's war on idolatry and the very destructive results of the pagan practices of the nations around Judah. His discernment and directives show a bent toward blindness and rebellion that rivaled even some of his most wicked predecessors.

Manasseh's disregard for past and present prophecy, positive and negative examples of the history of rise-and-fall in Judah and the removal of many previous occupants of Canaan due to vile practices screams loudly as warnings for leaders who may find pride creeping in and similar tendencies arising. Some revealing questions for 21st-century leaders in this regard may be: 1) Do you feel you are immune to problems and practices that have brought others down? 2) Do you find yourself justifying questionable activities because your success and position allow you to live "above" these parameters? 3) How focused are you on the direction and commands of ancient scriptural principles, especially when those seem to run contrary to popular opinion or societal standards? 4) How is "tolerance" defined when building your team and establishing organizational values? 5) What part of your personal self-worth is derived from constituents' applause and the amount of private financial compensation received?

No doubt the essence of these kinds of questions would have had immediate applicability to Manasseh had he been willing to face them squarely and honestly. May everyone who names the name of Christ, and especially those leading others, never turned a blinded eye to these warning signs around us!

Forgetting the Eternal: People Abused

Jesus taught many lessons related to His second coming and the culmination of this present age. One can find an occasion of this sort in Luke 12:35-48. A portion of this passage is especially revelatory related to the kinds of behaviors leaders manifest when an eternal perspective is lost. Jesus instructs,

> Who then is a faithful and wise steward, whom his master will make ruler over his household, to give them their portion of food in due season? Blessed is that servant whom his master will find so doing when he comes. Truly, I say to you that he will make him ruler over all that he has. But if that servant says in his heart, ' My master is delaying his coming,' and *begins to beat the male and female servants*, and to eat and drink and be drunk, the master of that servant will come on a day when he is not looking for him, and at an hour when he is not aware, and will cut him in two and appoint him his portion with the unbelievers. (12:42-46, italics mine)

"Stewards" (leaders responsible for others' property) trusted with the privilege of empowering other "servants" (employees, congregational constituents, family members, etc.) must be careful to keep an eternal focus to provide a climate conducive for all to accomplish God's will. Loss of a strong sense of accountability and eternal responsibility in the leader often results, per Jesus, in two very distinct and detrimental behaviors. It comes as no surprise to see both of these characterizing the leadership of Manasseh.

Sacrifice

When mentioning the term sacrifice, the willingness to allow illicit behaviors is not usually an initial picture that arises. However, when dealing with a covenant people with the calling to live among the nations as a sign of the power and presence of a holy God, permission toward promiscuity and the promotion of false gods yields what is tantamount to the sacrifice of those people on the altar of hedonism.

The biblical narrative is replete with mentions of the variety of practices instituted by Manasseh that not only tolerated but, in fact, celebrated behaviors that were strongly prohibited by God. Among the most heinous of these practices was the establishment of child sacrifice outside Jerusalem's walls in the Valley of Hinnom. This practice was most likely due to the adoption of the worship of the Canaanite god Molech and appeared to have been practiced regularly for a time, even by the king himself (2 Kings 21:6;16). Also provoking God to anger would be the prevalence of prohibited altars and unlawful offerings being offered both in the Temple and on "high places" across the nation. Once again, these were activities sanctioned by the king, with participation expected by the citizens.

While child sacrifice and visibly practiced idolatry and offerings are not usually occurrences in 21st century American leadership and culture, the spiritual counterparts to these ancient visible practices are very much alive. How many leaders come to the end of active organizational roles to look behind them to the burned bridges of relational disarray, health depletion, marriage dissolution, and children despite? What a sad day to see these "true riches" sacrificed to the gods of vocation, financial independence, adoration and accolades, and other forms of success-so-called? It is disturbing to know the "unlawful sacrifices" made on modern "high places" have come to haunt so many!

When a strong sense of the eternal is lost, often so are those things most important in this present life!

Syncretism

One significant insight is seen into the powerful and polluting activity of Manasseh when the biblical writer states that the king "seduced" the inhabitants of Judah into a place of disobedience to the law of God (2 Kings 21:9). The term seduce can translate several ways, including to cause to reel, to make to stagger, and to create a stupor like intoxication.[76] The persuasion of this wicked king so overwhelmed the people that prophetic warnings sent their way were ignored. They then gave heed to the persuasive but toxic leadership (so-called!) of the highly charismatic king.

Nothing can be truly seductive unless it is attractive. Attraction, of course, is in the eye of the beholder, but the force of any seduction stems from a sense of desire emanating from the seduced subject. It becomes evident that the seductive power behind the destructive impact of Manasseh was participation in and encouragement of an unbridled syncretism. By definition, syncretism is very simply the "combination of different forms of belief or practice."[77] While still allowing a form of Temple sacrifice and worship of Yahweh, the king effectively staggered the nation with the intoxicating effects of a syncretistic tolerance gone awry.

Interestingly, just a few decades after the reign of Manasseh, Jeremiah spoke of the same ills of false hope and security meant to substitute for real worship of the only true God. The prophet declares to those advocating idolatrous practices and ungodly alliances:

> …from the prophet even to the priest, Everyone deals falsely.
> They have also healed the hurt of My people slightly, saying,
> 'Peace, peace!' When there is no peace. Were they ashamed
> when they had committed abomination? No! there were not
> at all ashamed; Nor did they know how to blush. Therefore,
> they shall fall among those who fall; At the time I punish
> them, They shall be cast down, says the Lord (6:12b-15).

Similarly, while seeing the upcoming duress of impending captivity, Ezekiel speaks to prophetic leadership a strong word of rebuke for giving false hope through the seduction of the people (Ezekiel 13).

Both Jeremiah and Ezekiel were warning against the tendency and futility of attempting to put a <u>superficial dressing on a mortal wound</u>!

Some leaders in 21st-century contexts are deceived and deceiving others when proposing a syncretism of beliefs and values that deny the exclusivity of Jesus Christ as Lord (John 14:6) and by attempts to appease a demanding constituency (2 Tim. 4:1-5). This problem is not only found in church leadership but is active in any context where followers demand personal preferences and compromise of commitment. Christ-centered leaders must become increasingly aware of the desire of this world's system to "press you into its mold" (Rom. 12:1-2, Phillips) and stand firm on biblical foundations alone when intimidated by forces around them.

Regaining and maintaining an eternal perspective will help to keep syncretism and its adverse effects at bay as leaders stand strong against the intoxication it brings.

Repentance and Redemption

Shining like a diamond on the dark background of a jeweler's showcase is the eventual repentance of Manasseh and his corresponding attempt to right the wrongs he had created in Judah. The restoration of this otherwise wicked king seemed to require drastic measures and extremely difficult circumstances to find root.

While the nation of Judah begins to feel the impending danger of an eventual Babylonian invasion, their leader finds himself in a prison cell with virtually no hope for survival. Brought to his knees (literally and metaphorically), Manasseh cries out to God, in what must have been a genuine prayer of repentance. True to His merciful nature, God then brought a season of reprieve and redemption for the king and the land.

Three areas of supernatural intervention were necessary to restore this broken king to a place of true God-consciousness and desire for holiness. These same three are essential in any leader to keep their "eyes on the prize" and attention focused on things that are above (Col. 3:1).

God Does Something in Us

Manasseh certainly speaks to leaders that may have been deeply wounded (ever by the self-inflicted variety) but who are ready to repent as needed and get back in the arena. An internal work of healing and renewed vitality and desire for engagement is possible but comes only from a real work of Divine grace.

Though well-worn and much-quoted, the words of a former American president serve well as leaders tether their present leadership sails to eternal masts and, in doing so, resist becoming victim to the undertow of fear-induced, temporal, and debilitating diversions and inactivity. In his famous "Man in the Arena" speech delivered in Paris, France in April 1910, Theodore Roosevelt proclaimed:

> It is not the critic who counts; not the man who points out how the strong man stumbles, or where the doer of deeds could have done them better. The credit belongs to the man who is actually in the arena, whose face is marred by dust and sweat and blood; who strives valiantly; who errs, who comes short again and again, because there is no effort without error and shortcoming; but who does actually strive to do the deeds; who knows great enthusiasms, the great devotions; who spends himself in a worthy cause; who at the best knows in the end the triumph of high achievement, and who at the worst, if he fails, at least fails while daring greatly, so that his place shall never be with those cold and timid souls who neither know victory nor defeat.[78]

For Christ-centered leaders to stay ready for battle assignments from the King, an eternal perspective and repentance with restoration are standard equipment from the inside-out emanating from the merciful hand of God.

God Does Something For Us

The release of Manasseh from Babylonian prison is a powerful and very encouraging act of Divine intervention on behalf of the repentant king and the nation of Judah. There is not a better example to be found related to the biblical promise that "The king's heart is in the hand of the Lord, like the rivers of water; He turns it wherever He wishes" (Prov. 21:1).

God is sovereign in His activities both in heaven and on earth. Thus, a leader with eyes on eternity can be confident that the "King of kings and Lord of Lords" (Rev. 19:6) can work on their behalf in a manner that far surpasses the ability to plan, network, collaborate, ask, or even imagine (Eph. 3:20)! If failure, mistakes, and compromise have left you languishing in a "prison" of obscurity and uncertainty, you are only a prayer of true confession and repentance away from restoration and renewed productivity for His glory!

God Does Something through Us

The scripture records the final acts of Manasseh as characterized by both personal reformation and the attempted reformation of religious practices in Judah back to Yahweh's person and precepts. While this is undoubtedly a brighter ending to the story than may have been anticipated in earlier scenes of rebellion and evil, it appears that the efforts of the transformed king were too little too late for a lasting impact on the nation as a whole.

As mentioned before in this chapter, Manasseh's son, and successor Amon, took up his father's idolatrous ways upon taking the throne. Amon also caused the nation to revert to the pagan practices prominent in the nation before his father's restoration. It is not beyond the stretch of the imagination to see Manasseh restored as Judah's king but continually lamenting the years lost to flagrant disobedience and prideful practices.

Only God knows how many leaders in any generation have buried their faces in a pillow at night and soaked that with tears of remorse and regret over lost favor and God-designed opportunities. Perhaps Manasseh would say to all about repentance and redemption that later is better than never, but the earlier, the better... time is shorter than you think!

Final Thoughts

While penning this chapter and thinking again about that sand-sculpturing day on the beach, I have entered into some self-reflection related to the actual eternal fruit my present energies are producing. The fact that you are reading these words is an answer to prayer in that regard.

As a result of this reflection, I have begun to close all my letters with the phrase "With eternity in mind." Perhaps this will serve better than cordially, yours truly, sincerely, etc., in helping others gain or retain an eternal outlook. Its dawning is closer than we think!

Chapter Eleven – King Josiah – (640-609) 2 Kings 22-23; 2 Chronicles 34-35

Both the records of 2 Kings and 2 Chronicles begin their narrative of King Josiah with the positive compliment, "He did what was right in the eyes of the LORD and followed the ways of his father David, not turning aside to the right or to the left." At the tender age of only 8 years old, Josiah was installed as the King of Judah. Even though his father, Amon, was a bad leader, Josiah proved to be Judah's bright example in leadership. We will examine his reign based around three key age markers during his lifetime.

1. Josiah at Age 16

At 16 years old, Josiah began to seek the Lord. The positive mentoring, he received — most likely from his mother, priests, and court officials — yielded positive fruit. Four years later, when he was 20 years old, he began to purge the land of idolatry.

In times past, Judah experienced covenant renewal, and their leaders would remove idols. At other seasons, their faith wavered, and they slid back into pagan worship, reinstalling the previously removed idols. Josiah took the extra step in his reforms to pulverize the idols and scatter their ashes. He removed from Judah the zodiac worship and mediums.

Royal chariots that had been dedicated to the sun and placed at the entrance to the temple by previous Judean kings, but Josiah burned them. In March 2019, a seal was discovered in Jerusalem dating to the time of Josiah, that even mentions the court official Nathan-Melech, whose office was located nearby the sun chariots (2 Kgs. 23:11).[79]

Josiah did not stop with just the Judean region. The northern kingdom of Israel no longer existed as a nation since her fall to

Assyria in 722 B.C. With Assyria in decline, Josiah moved into the northern territory and continued his reform campaign. Numerous administrative stamps and inscriptions during this time are in harmony with Josiah's expansions to the west and north.[80]

The text informs us that Josiah personally went into these areas to remove idols. He even destroyed the high place at Bethel that Jeroboam I had erected more than three centuries earlier. Near the time of its original installation, a prophet approached Jeroboam I and prophesied that one day a man named Josiah, a descendent of the house of David, would demolish the altar (1 Kgs. 13). More than three centuries passed, but the word of the unnamed prophet endured until its fulfilment.

2. Josiah at Age 26

When Josiah was 26 years old, the priest Hilkiah discovered a copy of the book of the law. It is sad to think that all copies of this important document had previously been destroyed by corrupt leaders. This scroll was most likely the book of Deuteronomy. The book gives instructions on what a nation should do, what a nation should not do, and the results of which direction the nation chooses.

Hilkiah gave the scroll to Shaphan the scribe, who then took the manuscript to Josiah. A generation later, Jeremiah would record that Shaphan's son, Gemariah, continued in his father's footsteps as a royal scribe (Jer. 36:10). A seal mentioning both Shaphan and Gemariah has been discovered.[81]

The reading of the scroll had a profound effect on King Josiah. He tore his robe and brought the prophetess Huldah in for counsel. She confirmed that the nation of Judah was in serious trouble and must take immediate action. Therefore, the king embarked on an even more ambitious reform campaign. A public renewal of the covenant occurred, as well as Judah's greatest Passover celebration.

3. Josiah at Age 39

When Josiah was 39 years old, the Near East was experiencing dramatic changes. The Neo-Assyrian empire was nearing its end after three centuries of oppressive rule. The Neo-Babylonian empire was emerging under the capable leadership of Nabopolassar and his son, Nebuchadnezzar. By 612 B.C., the Assyrian capital city of Nineveh had fallen. The remaining Assyrian holdouts fled westward to Harran. By 609 B.C., Harran also fell to Babylon.

To add to this conflict, in 609 B.C., Pharaoh Necho II moved northward to assist the Assyrians. While Egypt gained her independence from Assyria years earlier, Necho II assumed Egypt would be better off supporting a known empire than an evolving one. Necho had to traverse through Judah, and this is where King Josiah entered this drama.

For reasons not given, Josiah confronted Necho's army at the Jewish stronghold of Megiddo in 609 B.C. Perhaps Josiah's reason centered on the long, tyrannical history of Assyria with Judah. Certainly, Josiah would not endorse Egypt's support of Assyria. Regardless, Necho did his best to persuade Josiah to depart. The record in 2 Chronicles endorses the Pharaoh's admonitions to Josiah as being correct counsel. In the ensuing battle, Josiah disguised himself but was wounded by the Egyptian archers. His soldiers hurried him away to Jerusalem where he died from his wounds. He was only 39 years old.

Conclusion on King Josiah

In somber tones, the narrative of King Josiah concludes. He is respectfully buried in the tombs of the Judean kings with full honors. The prophet Jeremiah wrote laments about this amazing leader. The laments were sung by choirs and became an annual tradition among the Jewish people. He is permanently honored for his many acts of devotion. No earthly king exceeded him.

Application - Chapter 11 - Josiah - The Worth of the Word

Serendipity…

What a beautiful word with an even more beautiful meaning. According to various dictionary renderings, the term serendipity refers to "the aptitude or occurrence of discovering something valuable and desirable by accident."[82] Perhaps there is no better word to describe one of the most significant events in King Josiah's life.

The scripture records that Josiah, at age 26, began a major renovation campaign for the Temple in Jerusalem (2 Kings 22:3-8). Before his reign, previous kings (including his father) had taken Judah down the path of increased idolatry and paganistic worship. Thus, the Temple, with its physical furnishings and spiritual significance, had been allowed to deteriorate and essentially be left unattended. Some have even suggested the Temple itself had become a waste-dump of sorts allowing Jerusalem residents to dispose of their garbage there without having to make the trek down and back up the steep Temple Mount en route to the city landfill!

During the renovation efforts on the Temple, a remarkable discovery came to light. Workers preparing to make much-needed improvements on the building's internal structure serendipitously uncovered a copy of The Book of the Law. This Book was delivered to Hilkiah, the High Priest, and then to Shaphan the Scribe to be presented and read before King Josiah. Josiah's reaction of alarm and repentance when listening to the words of the Law was completely in character with the king's desire to bring the nation back to a place of favor with God (2 Kings 22:9-20).

Finding and giving heed to the Word of God grants Josiah further motivation to cleanse the nation of its idolatrous bent and allows this monarch several more years of prosperity in Judah (2 Kings 23:1-24). Though this favor would not last beyond Josiah's reign, it is significant that respect for the Word and corresponding acts of spiritual renewal gained this king the following biblically recorded honor: "Now before him there was no king like him, who turned to the Lord with all his heart, with all his soul, and with all his might, according to all the Law of Moses; nor after him did any arise like him" (2 Kings 23:25).

By now, it should be evident that what appears to be, from the natural vantage point, a serendipitous advantage and turn of events is actually the sovereignty of a loving God at work to bring restoration to His people! Could it be that the same gracious God desires to do a similar work with individuals, families, nations, and the world in the 21st century? If so, might this be anchored on the same foundation as the revival of Josiah... a rediscovery of the Word of God? If so, this "return to the Word" will undoubtedly be an intentional emphasis and focus of leaders who recognize the "worth of the Word." These leaders will not leave this critical issue of discovery to serendipity, chance, or wishful thinking!

The Worth of the Word

The Bible is replete with passages concerning scripture's value and power as the revealed Word of God. Just a few of these references suffice to see the Word as describes in such life-giving ways as milk (1 Peter 2:2), fire (Jeremiah 23:29), living bread (John 6:47-51), and water for cleansing (Ephesians 5:25-26). No wonder the Psalmist proclaims the Word as "more to be desired than gold... (and) sweeter than the honeycomb" (Psalm 19:9-10)!

Two of the most poignant of these mentions describe the Word as "light" and "incorruptible (imperishable; indestructible) seed."

Light

Among the many biblical references to the Bible as light, one of the most significant is found in the words of the Psalmist when declaring a source of light that will bring illumination to the darkness: "The entrance of Your words gives light; It gives understanding to the simple" (Ps. 119:130). As society is churning in the confusion of anarchy, polarization, and desperation, how encouraging to know there is a source of light that can bring clarity in the chaos and calm amid calamities! God's Word can powerfully penetrate and overcome the prevailing darkness and difficulties of very uncertain days.

Have you ever wondered how generally well-educated and sometimes high-ranking people can vehemently argue for the most ridiculous things and fight for absolutely ludicrous agendas in challenging times like ours? Have you ever been caught off guard by the animosity experienced from the words and behavior of some who, except for the volatile issues proposed, lead relatively normal and peaceful lives? I think I may have found at least part of the answer to this dilemma in, of all places, an underground cavern…

An Island Cave

Several years ago, while preaching at various churches on the beautiful Caribbean island of Barbados, some locals pastors treated my wife and me to a tour of some underground caverns in that country. I remember placing my hard hat on, entering the tram that would start us on our journey underground, and being excited about both the sights to see and the drop in temperature offering some relief from the tropical climate above ground. As the tram descended, it eventually dropped us off for the walking portion of the experience. With the assistance of a very experienced guide, we carefully navigated the narrow caverns and illuminated stalactites and stalagmites contained therein. What a beautiful and exciting adventure indeed.

However, the guide stopped us during the tour and asked that we all turn off any lights on our hats or being carried in our hands. After doing so, the guide then extinguished all other light sources in the cave, leaving us in what he described as "total darkness." No light whatsoever was discernable, and I remember later describing the darkness as something "so thick you could almost feel it." After about a minute or so of allowing us to experience the sensation of total darkness, our guide then took a small flashlight out. It beamed our attention to a small stream of water running alongside the path we were standing on. In this stream were some fish, all white and with strangely glowing pink eyes. The guide explained that all these fish were white because the cavern's lack of light has prevented any pigmentation from occurring on their bodies. They were all also blind. The lack of light had prevented the development of optical abilities and left them without the ability to see.

The guide went on to drive the point home to us by giving us the following "facts": 1) If you were to spend a short amount of time in this context of total darkness, you would also soon go blind; 2) But, it would not really matter, he went on to say, because before you lost your sight, you would have already lost your mind! While I am not sure either of these interesting points can be scientifically verified, I will always remember the connection presented between light, sight, and potential insanity!

Could it be, friends, that the lack of sight in our society and the seemingly insane ideas propagated are the direct results of a lack of light? Might this further be explained by a depreciation of the value of the Word of God (society wide as well as in the church!)? Might the mindless arguments and activities being experienced directly relate to a "darkness" that has blinded eyes, stolen reason, and animalized a culture?

If so, what great news to reminded that "the Word of the Lord brings light!" With light, it can also restore societal sanity and sight, giving hope to a generation apprehensive about what is to come. Oh, let there be light!

Incorruptible Seed

Another powerful metaphor describing the Word is that of "incorruptible seed" (1 Peter 1:23). The term incorruptible (imperishable; indestructible) in this passage is set in contrast to other "corruptible" (changing) things that men tend to place their security and even religious confidence in (cp. 1 Peter 1:18-20). In a time like ours where so little seems to have lasting value and long-term significance, Peter tells us the Word is a trustworthy foundation for confident living both presently and forever because it is "forever seed" that will stand the test of time!

Another story from one of my favorites places to visit may serve well to bring this point home.

A Treasure Museum

My wife and I enjoy taking short road trips (1-3 days) from time to time to see some of the more "local" places of interest. One of those spots we love to visit is the Mel Fisher Maritime Museum in Key West, Florida.[83] This museum is a fascinating place to explore and learn about this modern-day treasure hunter's adventures and some of the "booty" their team has been able to excavate from the sea's floor.

One of the shipwrecks sought out and eventually discovered was the Spanish galleon, Nuestra Señora de Atocha. This ship sunk in 1622 off the shores of what is now South Florida after being caught in a hurricane. The story of the 16-year search for this shipwreck, the challenges and tragedies experienced during that adventure, and the eventual discovery and excavation is worthy of any treasure hunter's interest. July 20, 1985... it must have been quite a day!

> On July 20, 1985, Kane Fisher, captain of the salvage vessel Dauntless, sent a triumphant message to his father's headquarters, "Put away the charts; we've found the main pile!" Ecstatic crew members described the find as looking like a reef of silver bars. Within days, the shipper's marks on the bars were matched to the Atocha's cargo manifest, confirming Kane's triumphant claim. At long last, the wreck's "motherlode" had been found. The excavation of the so-called "shipwreck of the century" then began.[84]

As can be imagined, Treasure Salvors, Fisher's company, recovered incredible treasure from the Atocha wreck. Among this "booty" were large quantities of various artifacts like plates, eating utensils, personal items, etc. Also, as might be expected, large amounts of gold (chains, bars, coins, etc.), silver, and precious jewels were among the items extracted from the ship's waiting ruins. Just a few years ago, we were at the museum and found that a pay-to-find-treasure diver had recently uncovered another gold bar that week when visiting the underwater sight. This find was at least 20+ years from the initial discovery in 1985!

Another example of the incredible wealth found in this adventure would be the discovery dated May 28, 1986. Having been called "the day it rained emeralds," it was this date that is marked as the uncovering of the "emerald city" hoard of green jewels, about 2300 in the count, and with just one uncut gem weighing in at over 77 carats!

However, despite all the wealth described from gold, silver, jewels, and precious and irreplaceable artifacts (this is a list that could go on and one), in my estimation, none of these things are the most important find from the Atocha. What appeared to be a relatively inconsequential mining maneuver yielded a treasure that brings the mention of this event to this chapter on the value of the Word. While excavating the Spanish galleon treasures, seed caught between boards of the ship's infrastructure was extracted from the ocean's floor along with other pieces of the wreck. While no one initially thought much about these remains of some long-gone plant life, after a few days in the sunlight, these seeds began to sprout! Yes, my friend, after 323 years "buried" in the salty waters on the ocean floor, these seeds had the resilience to not only survive but to sprout when placed in the right environment. Oh, the power of the seed.

When learning about this marvelous seed from the Atocha, my mind immediately went to the passage in 1 Peter 1:23 that opened this chapter section. If God has put enough resilience in a natural seed to survive a watery grave for over three centuries, how much more "incorruptibility" is there in the Word of God as seed that has eternal power and purpose! Three principles are especially noteworthy from this realization.

First, this should encourage us as to the presence of the Word-seed in lives and places where it is planted, even when the fruit is not yet visible. Regardless of what rebellion and disobedience have piled on top of it, the seed is still present and potent. Placed in the right conditions, it will sprout as planned! Second, this should urge every Christ-follower to make sure they are personally planting incorruptible seed into their personal lives for strength, direction, protection, and wisdom to be an effective Kingdom ambassador (2 Corinthians 5:20). Third, every leader should be warned of the undertow to push other sources of information and inspiration to the forefront when training others, often to the exclusion of the only thing in the world that is truly "incorruptible seed." Do all in your power within your leadership context parameters to provide the opportunity for those on your team to be filled with the wisdom and strength that only eternal seed can offer.

The Worth of the Word – A Suggestion

For this final thought on this chapter dealing with the worth of the Word, Psalm 119 is a place one might want to dedicate a time of devotional study. This passage is the longest chapter in the Bible, with the entire chapter having to do with benefits one might expect from being a hearer and doer of the Word.

Twenty-two sections constitute this Psalm, each representing one letter of the Hebrew alphabet. Each stanza (division) has eight verses, and each of the verses in the specific stanza begins with the Hebrew letter that heads the section. Just a little overview information to emphasize that this Psalm was put together with great care (and Divine inspiration, of course) to provide the reader with some well-structured principles related to the Word's work and worth!

My suggestion would be to take a "slow walk" through each of the stanzas for 22 days and spend time discovering, highlighting, and meditating on the benefits prescribed by that section that day. The results of this devotional exploration and exercise will also be well worth sharing in family devotions, pulpit messages, one-on-one conversations, Bible studies in various contexts, etc.

Happy hunting!

The Clutter

Remember Josiah. His finding the Word was the result of serendipity but to which he responded well. It paid off big time! The removal of a lot of clutter was necessary to make the "chance" moment happen.

While we do not depend on serendipity to bring us a Word-discovery, there is little doubt that our commitment to draw closer to God through the Word will also require some deep digging through some loud noises, crowded agendas, and unending diversions. Pressing through will be well worth the effort!

Chapter Twelve – Kings Jehoahaz, Jehoiakim, Jehoiachin, Zedekiah – (609-587) - 2 Kings 23; 2 Chronicles 26

Josiah had four sons, with Johanan listed as the oldest. Since he is no longer in the picture, we assume he died prematurely. After Josiah's death, the last 20 years of the Judean kingdom were ruled by three of Josiah's sons and one of his grandsons. The reigns of these four kings are combined here in an effort to simplify a rather complex period of history. We have listed the last four kings in relation to Josiah and in relation to their reigning order.

1. Josiah's Youngest Son - Jehoahaz (Shallum) – (609)

Upon Josiah's death, the people of the land took his youngest son, Jehoahaz, and made him king. The reason why Josiah's youngest son was chosen is not given. Perhaps he was the strongest leader, or the least pro-Assyrian of the three remaining sons of Josiah. Both the sons Jehoahaz and Zedekiah had the same mother.

After only 3 months, Pharaoh Necho II removed Jehoahaz and placed his oldest half-brother, Jehoiakim, on the throne. For a brief period of time, Egypt forced Judah into a vassal state under Egyptian rule. The last chapter of Jeremiah gives two dates that initially seem to conflict with each other. Instead, one date is based on the Egyptian chronology and the second on the Babylonian method. Both dates are in harmony as both nations of Egypt and Babylon largely controlled this region. Little is known about Jehoahaz except that he was exiled to Egypt by Necho II where he finished out his days. The account in 2 Kings indicates that he did not continue his father's reforms during his brief reign.

2. Josiah's Oldest Son – Jehoiakim (Eliakim) – (609-598)

After Pharaoh Necho II deposed Jehoahaz, he placed Josiah's oldest remaining son, Eliakim, as king. Necho installed the Judean king with the new throne name of Jehoiakim. The pharaoh also enacted a heavy tribute upon Judah. King Jehoiakim was forced to heavily tax the people to meet the tribute requirements. By 605 B.C., Egypt was defeated by the Babylonians at the famous battle of Carchemish. The last vestige of the Assyrian empire had also fled across the Euphrates to Carchemish and joined the Egyptian troops. With both Assyria and Egypt defeated at Carchemish, the Neo-Babylonian empire dominated the Near East for the next 70 years.

Jehoiakim reigned for 11 years. The book of Jeremiah gives us our most informed view of this disastrous leader. Jeremiah faithfully proclaimed good counsel to Jehoiakim, but the foolish king rejected every admonition, burned Jeremiah's writings, and constantly persecuted the prophet. A number of individuals mentioned in Jeremiah have been discovered in archaeology. Of particular interest is Baruch, Jeremiah's scribe, and Jerahmeel, the king's son.[85]An additional prophet named Uriah ben Shemaiah was killed by Jehoiakim (Jer. 26:20-23).

Babylon besieged the Judean region. Jehoiakim had to pay tribute to Babylon with the treasury and some royal family members were held as hostages. Jehoiakim was constantly out of touch with reality. In the midst of heavy Babylonian occupation and taxation, he foolishly chose that timeframe to build himself a spatial palace at his people's expense. Jeremiah reminded the king that his father, Josiah, had modeled justice and righteousness by pleading the cause of the afflicted and needy. Such leadership, Jeremiah said, was an indication that a leader truly knew the Lord.

Jehoiakim foolishly rebelled against Babylon and realigned himself with Egypt. Jeremiah prophesied that, "the king would die prematurely with none of the people lamenting his death. Additionally, he would have no formal burial, but his body would be cast into an open field." Nebuchadnezzar fulfilled Jeremiah's prophecy. Jehoiakim was apprehended at the end of the Babylonian siege. Initially, he was to be taken to Babylon as a prisoner. Instead, he was put to death. According to Josephus, Nebuchadnezzar had Jehoiakim's body tossed over the Jerusalem walls into an open field.

3. Josiah's Grandson – Jehoiachin (Jeconiah)

After the death of Jehoiakim, his son Jehoiachin was placed on the throne. He ruled a mere 3 months. Nebuchadnezzar took Jehoiachin, his entire household, and many others into exile in 597 B.C. Among those in exile was the prophet Ezekiel, whose book largely anchors the 597exile date as a cornerstone for his prophetic timeline.

From 1899–1917, German archaeologists conducted major excavations on the ancient city of Babylon.[86] Near the Ishtar Gate, the archaeologist discovered an underground record vault with numerous tablets. On one of the tablets, King Jehoiachin is mentioned as being taken into exile. The record lists the rations allotted for him and his family. Jeremiah prophesied that none of Jehoiachin's descendants would ever sit on the throne of Israel (Jer. 22:28–30). This prophecy was fulfilled.

4. Josiah's Middle Son – Zedekiah (Mattaniah)

In 597 B.C., Nebuchadnezzar removed Jehoiachin as king and replaced him with his uncle, Mattaniah. The new king's throne name was changed to Zedekiah. The Babylonian Chronicle documents Nebuchadnezzar's conquest of Jerusalem in 597 B.C., his removal of the reigning Judean king (Jehoiachin), and the installation of a new king of Nebuchadnezzar's choosing (Zedekiah).[87] During Zedekiah's 11-year reign, the prophet Jeremiah consistently gave good counsel to the king; however, Zedekiah rarely listened. The prophet Jeremiah stated Zedekiah's final epitaph as, "He did evil in the sight of the Lord" (Jer. 52:2–3).

Against Jeremiah's advice, Zedekiah rebelled against Nebuchadnezzar. In the ensuing Babylonian siege of Jerusalem, Zedekiah, his family, and his officials fled Jerusalem. They were overtaken in the plains of Jericho. Zedekiah's captors escorted him on the long journey to Nebuchadnezzar's northern headquarters in the city of Riblah in Syria. Nebuchadnezzar had all Zedekiah's sons executed before him, his eyes were blinded, and then he was taken to Babylon in chains. The last Judean king remained a prisoner until his death. Both Jeremiah and Ezekiel had prophesied this outcome for Zedekiah (Jer. 32:1-5; Ez. 12:8-13).

Conclusion on the Kings Jehoahaz, Jehoiakim, Jehoiachin, Zedekiah

After the fall of Jerusalem in 587 B. C., the city was plundered and razed to the ground.[88] Two-thirds of the population died during the Babylonian siege. The one-third remaining were exiled to Babylon. Nebuchadnezzar left only a small number of farmers to maintain the vineyards and land.

Hopelessness set into the Jewish community. All seemed lost. They lost their independence, leaders, treasure, temple, and most of their population. Into this dark backdrop shines the prophets. Their cumulative messages predict a timeline for the exile, a return from exile, a removal of idolatry from the people, and a new temple. Most importantly, they foresaw the coming of the ultimate Judean king, the Messiah. Hope remained.

Application - Chapter 12 - Jehoahaz, Jehoiachin, and Zedekiah - Weak Knees and Unstable Footing

Astronauts and space travel fascinate me. Not that I aspire to be directly involved, mind you, nor am I a "Trekkie" by any stretch of the imagination. However, from John Glenn's inaugural flight to Neil Armstrong's famous "small step… giant leap" and the more present-day reinstitution of the United States space program, I am a mesmerized fan.

In conversation with a colleague, it was just recently that the discussion of a very critical aspect of astronaut training arose. This training emphasis has to do with the controlling of intense symptoms akin to severe motion sickness. Technically labeled SAS (Space Adaptation Syndrome), attempting to conquer this potentially devastating problem (think of vomiting inside a helmet and spacesuit!) has required the assistance of experts from a variety of disciplines, including the notable contributions from Dr. Patricia Cowlings. Dr. Cowlings, an aerospace psycho-physiologist and the first American woman trained as an astronaut, did most of her scientific research at NASA. Here she developed and patented a physiological training system called Autogenic-Feedback Training Exercise (AFTE). This system enables participants to exercise voluntary self-control of up to 24 bodily responses, including several imbalances that cause motion and space sickness. Dr. Cowlings, considered one of the world's top experts in motion sickness, has thus earned the term of endearment from colleagues, the Baroness of Barf!

During years of research and experimentation, Dr. Cowling discovered several factors contributing to SAS (and applicable to other forms of motion sickness). The weakness and instability brought on by these factors resulted in the inability to carry on necessary routines and tasks and, in extreme situations, could result in death. In the following sections, we will examine some parallels between causes of motion sickness and the dysfunction and disorientation of Judah's final kings.

A Lack of Grounding

SAS and other forms of severe motion sickness are often the results of a lack of solid grounding. The human body functions best with a sense of equilibrium resulting from stable footing and corresponding chemical balances. With the loss of gravitational pull and change in g-forces in space, astronauts experience difficulty maintaining proper spatial orientation. Realizing where they are, what direction is what, and keeping a sense of focus are all adversely affected, and internal "turmoil" results. In other words, when a strong foundation and pull toward stability is removed, one has trouble discerning the who, what, where, and even the why of the next move!

There can be little doubt as we look at the final three kings of Judah, Jehoahaz, Jehoiachin, and Zedekiah, that a severe disequilibrium plagued their decisions and destinies. A lack of strong commitment and trust in God and a proper value system related to this foundation is evident as all three kings experienced indecision, accommodation, and allegiance vacillation to the point of personal and national decay, eventually to the point of no return. A leader's firm and non-negotiable personal values are the starting point of creating a culture where people around them will feel security, ownership, and direction. When a leader succumbs to the pressure of compromise and accommodation, this is always the "beginning of the end" related to personal and organizational effectiveness!

In some very rigorous and longitudinal studies, researchers Jim Kouzes and Barry Posner explored leadership practices and credibility characteristics that produce desired organizational results over the long haul. This research reveals five exemplary practices leaders most often are involved in when they are functioning at their best: 1) Model the way; 2) Inspire a shared vision; 3) Challenge the process; 4) Enable others to act, and 5) Encourage the heart.[89] Additionally, four major characteristics perceived by followers in their leaders lend toward a climate of credibility and remain consistent over three decades of inquiry: 1) Honesty, 2) Forward-looking, 3) Inspiring, and 4) Competent.[90] Quite noteworthy within these two lists is the inclusion of expectations founded on personal authenticity and bedrock values. A leader's <u>honesty</u> (authenticity and transparency are implied, not just truth-telling) and willingness to <u>role-model</u> values and expectations still serve as crucial components in providing an organizational atmosphere where all can thrive.

Attempts to accommodate fluctuating societal norms and frequently vacillating, as a result, will quickly erode what foundational practices and characteristics built only on solid foundational values can construct. Values founded on absolutes from an objective source of truth are the 21st-century leaders' best friend and ultimate bedrock for impact and effectiveness.

A Lack of Orientation

According to the Oxford Reference overview on sensory conflict theory, nausea and general disorientation experienced in motion sickness are due to a confusion of information received by different systems of the body. This reference states, "A proposed explanation for motion sickness according to which passive movement creates a mismatch between information relating to orientation and movement supplied by the visual and the vestibular systems, and it is this mismatch that induces feelings of nausea."[91] Dr. Cowling would agree when interviewed by Washington Post reporter David Wallis several years ago. When asked by Mr. Wallis, "What triggers motion sickness?" she replied, "A conflict of information between different sensory systems. Unfamiliar information can cause the eye and ear to tell you different things."[92]

The scripture also grants some significant and similar insight into this issue when James declares, "A double-minded man is *unstable* in all his ways." (James 1:8 KJV, italics mine) The context of this passage gives the picture of a man succumbing to motion sickness (seasick, 1:6) and thus unable to think properly or move with unwavering balance. The Greek word used for double-minded, dipsychos, actually sets forth the idea of "vacillation in opinion or purpose" due to conflicting information from two (di) minds (psychos).[93] James goes on to express the counter-productive nature of this vacillation as he warns, "That person should not expect to receive anything from the Lord" (1:7 NIV).

If the essence of leadership is making the right things happen for the right group and the right time, then vacillation caused by the inability to sort through conflicting information is a sure killer of a leader's purpose and effectiveness. This principle transcends time, is universal in application, and holds true whether speaking of ancient Judean kings unstable in their allegiances and activities or referring to modern leadership contexts. Progress always suffers when the way forward cannot be discerned through the dense fog of confusion and conflicting information.

Personal Grounding and Reorientation

Chameleons are prevalent in my yard and are quite beautiful creatures. Watching these amazing lizards change colors to blend into their surroundings is fascinating. However, "chameleonitis" (my coined term) is neither beautiful nor fascinating when it infects a leader's personal and professional perceptions and activities. Chameleonitis in leadership is ugly and deadly.

Say! … Did you hear about the chameleon that fell into a box of crayons? It exploded! Okay… that's funny.

Say!… Did you hear about the multitude of leaders in the 21st century who think that success can be found by trying to gather popular opinions and construct their lives and leadership accordingly? They are flaming-out and resigning by the thousands every month… frustrated, exasperated, and often blaming themselves for not "having what it takes." Okay… that's not funny; it's heartbreaking.

Perhaps a quick reflection from my personal research can help nail down the final section of this chapter. While working on my doctoral dissertation (Enhancing Leader Credibility in Church

Leadership Trainees: Effective Mentoring Practices, 2007), a portion of the research was gathered from a group of college-aged ministry candidates who were isolated for inquiry through a quantitative measurement utilizing a well-established leadership instrument. After selecting this sample group, information was collected through a series of open-ended questions, with responses submitted through questionnaires and personal interviews.

One of the focal areas in questioning these ministry trainees related to the perceived credibility of a prominent leader whose proximity and position had allowed for significant influence and impact on all of the trainees. With absolutely no priming or interaction among the participants during the inquiry, posing a similar open-ended question as follows began the qualitative data gathering: "What characteristic about this leader most positively impacted you?" The answer I received to this question was something I never anticipated. The overwhelming majority of the trainees questioned answered that question with something akin to: "He did not try to be like us!" In other words, this mentor/leader was comfortable being himself and did not feel his influence was dependent on trying to dress, communicate, impress, and otherwise conform to the customs of this younger group of protégés.

Though completely unprepared for this response, I made a deep mental note. How counter-productive it becomes when a leader becomes overly sensitive to a group/culture/expectation, etc., and, in doing so, lose the moorings of their own identities, calling, and personal authenticity. Operating under the taskmasters of conformity, image, and vacillation will never catapult a leader and their organization forward. Instead, it will become the straight jacket that will eventually paralyze their purpose and suffocate their influence!

Kings of Judah, astronauts with NASA, and leaders of all types are subject to the adverse effects of "motion sickness."

In turbulent times with great uncertainty ahead, leaders everywhere must take time to reflect and seriously recalibrate. Questions too seldom revisited need addressing to provide a fresh sense of self-knowledge and purpose: Who am I? Why am I? Who are we? What is our real purpose? What is my/our legacy? Is my/our impact of any eternal significance? Self-inquiries like these can help us approach days ahead with a greater sense of foundational stability and directional orientation.

Epilogue - Doing Right in the Sight of the Lord

You have just completed a journey through history that clearly shows that, although technology and culture change, many things never do, and one of those is what it takes to be a great leader. Each of the kings we studied had an opportunity to make a difference. Each of them also had challenges to overcome. Yet, each king chose to handle the challenges and opportunities differently. Some led Judah to seasons of fruitfulness and peace. Others made choices that eventually destroyed their nation.

You can read a book like this with a natural curiosity to learn more about human history. You can approach it to gain information about the Bible. Yet, we never want to fall into the trap Jesus' half-brother James wants us about in his letter. Be careful not to look in the mirror and forget what you look like. Look at yourself and your leadership as you reflect on the lessons from these kings. As James went on the write, "But one who looks intently at the perfect law, the law of liberty, and abides by it, not having become a forgetful hearer but an effectual doer, this man will be blessed in what he does" (James 1:25, NASB). These words ring with those the editor of the Chronicles of the Kings of Israel and Judah wrote to summarize the reigns of the good kings of Judah, "He did right in the sight of the LORD AND walked in the ways of his father David and did not turn aside to the right or the left" (II Chronicles 34:2). These life lessons still apply today, perhaps more now than ever in our turbulent days and uncertain future. Do what God sees as right, and you will be blessed in all you do.

Charles and Sam gave us some clear direction as to what doing right in God's sight as leaders mean from their study of these Judean kings. Some of Judah's kings were outstanding leaders who followed God and their nation prospered as a result. Others have gone record as "doing evil in the sight of the LORD." The number one difference between these good and evil rulers is what they did with their private lives. Indeed, the decisions they made on behalf of the nation had a huge impact. Still, the chroniclers who recorded their stories for us in Kings and Chronicles' books continually refer to personal and faith-based obedience as the determining factor in their reigns. Those who worshipped the LORD faithfully in their hearts and lives were the ones recorded as good kings.

Although this faith in the good kings started in their hearts and personal worship, they inspired their nation to worship, and they were not afraid to remove false worship of idols and high places. Putting the LORD first in all things remained their priority. In contrast, most of the kings recorded as evil were noted as worshipping idols as the most defining trait of their lead times.

Our secular world does not usually celebrate faith in its celebrities and leaders, but this does not mean God's standard has changed. The Prophet Hanani's words are more accurate than ever. "The eyes of the LORD run to and fro throughout the whole earth, to give strong support to those whose heart is blameless toward him" (II Chronicles 16:9, ESV). May we never be caught seeking the power, glory, wealth, and fame leadership rather than the God who calls and equips us to lead.

Sam and Charles showed us many habits we can integrate into our personal lives and our leadership to see real fruitfulness. We can learn from Rehoboam's negative example to appreciate and listen to all generations' leaders when faced with challenges and significant decisions. Asa's model teaches us to humbly listen to those around us and carefully discern what God might be saying. Jehoram and Athaliah's hostile attitudes warn us against the risk of trying to overcompensate for our insecurity. Joash provides a beautiful example of the importance of finding wise and godly mentors, especially in our early years of leadership. In Chapter 6, Sam gave us an enormous life lesson from Amaziah on the importance of rest to finish well over the long term. If you have not already started, begin now to develop the habits of diverting daily, withdrawing weekly, and abandoning annually.

The recurring theme of leadership succession showed up again in the story of Uzziah. As it is often said, there is no success without a successor. Who comes after you will tell your story. What will they say? What if what you have done will remain?

Jotham's courage was contrasted by his son Ahaz's lack of courage. The Holy Spirit's empowering enabled Hezekiah to see the undreamed-of victory in the face of almost certain defeat. The contrast of Josiah's turning to God's Word contrasted with his evil father and grandfather, forgetting what matters when we adopt an eternal perspective. The last four kings demonstrate the importance of staying steady in turbulent times. It was unfortunate for their whole nation they did not follow the example of their father and grandfather Josiah in that faithfulness.

Despite the tragic end to the Kingdom of Judah with the Babylonian Conquest of 586 BC, we have many good things to learn from these kings. In contrast to most ancient empires, the Davidic Dynasty lasted for nearly four hundred years. By comparison, the Northern Kingdom of Israel changed dynasties eight times in just over two hundred years, and none of its kings are on record as good leaders. In purely economic terms, though, the Northern Kingdom of Israel should have been the one to thrive. It had more land, and that land was much more fertile and arable than Judah's land. That lesson still lives on for us: What you have is not nearly as important as what you do with it. We must be careful our assets don't become liabilities.

Another risk to avoid is assuming we can keep what we inherit. In contrast to the Northern kings, many Judean kings went on record as fair and doing right in the Lord's sight. Yet, good kings' children rarely followed their example of faith when they took the throne. Every generation must start fresh with its foundation of faith. We cannot trust in our predecessors' confidence and success. God measures each of us by our standards.

We also need to learn that starting well does not guarantee to finish well. King Asa's reign began well with a significant faith-filled victory over the Ethiopian army and a clearing away of idols. Yet, by the end of his 41-year long reign, he grew weak in both faith and will and paid the Aramean army to intimidate his rival King Baasha in Israel instead of trusting in the LORD as he did when he was younger. God rebuked him, and both he and his whole nation suffered for his lack of faith. King Hezekiah was another who started well. He rededicated the temple and restored true worship in Judah. His bold leadership and trust in God enabled Judah to overcome the previously undefeatable Assyrian Empire. The hard work of preparation enabled Jerusalem to survive a siege, and his conviction in God saw a miraculous deliverance from the world's mightiest army at that point. Yet faith shifted to arrogant overconfidence, even boastfully showing his treasures to the empire that would ultimately destroy the Kingdom of Judah - Babylon.

Yet, we saw that it is possible to both start well and end well. King Josiah has no record of wrongdoing. He inherited a very troubled kingdom from his short-reigning father Amon and long-reigning grandfather Manasseh, both of whom have been recorded for ages as doing evil in the sight of the Lord. Rather than succumbing to the pattern of what he saw in them, Josiah turned to the LORD with all of his heart. According to that Law, he restored the Law of God to the central place in society, and he brought everyone to worship in Jerusalem. Even today, our achievements will not be determined by what we inherit. We can choose to start well, and we can decide to finish well. Maintaining faithful obedience day after and taking decisive action to lead people in the right direction can give us a lasting legacy, as well. I pray your eternal record will bear the words, "This one did right in the sight of the Lord never turning aside to the right or the left."

Alan Ehler, D.Min

Endnotes

1   Hallo, William W., and K. Lawson Younger. *Context of Scripture.* Leiden: Brill, 2003. 2. 124.

2   Ussishkin, D., "Lachish," *The Oxford Encyclopedia of Archaeology in the Near East*, 3:317-23.

3   Pritchard, James B. *The Ancient Near East: Supplementary Texts and Pictures Relating to the Old Testament: Consisting of Supplementary Materials for The Ancient Near East in Pictures and Ancient Near Eastern Texts.* Princeton, New Jersey: Princeton University Press, 1969. 242-243.

4   Broekman, G. P. F., R. J. Demaree, and O. E. Kaper. The Libyan Period in Egypt: Historical and Cultural Studies into the 21st-24th Dynasties : Proceedings of a Conference at Leiden University, 25-27 October 2007. Leiden: Nederlands instituut voor het Nabije Oosten, 2009.

5   Pitard, Wayne Thomas. *Ancient Damascus.* Winona Lake: Ind, 1987. 138-144.

6   Chuck, Elizabeth. "Bob Ebeling, Engineer Who Predicted Space Shuttle Challenger Explosion, Dies," NBC News, March 24, 2016. https://www.nbcnews.com/news/us-news/bob-ebeling-engineer-who-predicted-space-shuttle-challenger-explosion-dies-n544926. Accessed 6/15/ 2020.

7   "Report of the Presidential Commission on the Space Shuttle Challenger Accident," United States Government Printing Office, 1986. https://er.jsc.nasa.gov/seh/explode.html. Accessed 01/27/21.

8   https://www.oringsusa.com/html/space_shuttle.html. Accessed 01/27/21.

9   O'Neil, John R. *The Paradox of Success.* New York: Putnam, 1994.

10   Bratskeir, Kate. "So Much Perfectly Edible Produce Is Wasted Every Year, Simply Because It's Ugly," The Huffington Post, May 19, 2015. https://www.huffpost.com/entry/food-waste-ugly-fruits-and-vegs-dont-judge_n_7309432. Accessed June 16, 2020

11   Interestingly, Jehoshaphat, Asa's son, seemed to learn a good lesson about disregarding what others may perceive to be a consistent naysayer. Though he did participate, like his father, in ill-advised alliances, he was at least willing to seek out and give heed to the genuine prophetic voice of Micaiah, those that voice was in the

extreme minority (1/401) among the "yes-men" of Ahab, King of Israel. See 2 Chron. 18.

12   De Pree, Max. *Leadership Is An Art*. New York: Currency Doubleday (Reprint edition), 2004. p. 11.

13   Mark, Jorie. "The Truth About Mike Pence's Policy Not to Dine Alone With Women," The List, August 23, 2020. https://www.thelist.com/239242/the-truth-about-mike-pences-policy-not-to-dine-alone-with-women/. Accessed 02/14/2021.

14   Myra, Harold, & Shelley, Marshall. *The Leadership Secrets of Billy Graham*. Grand Rapids, MI: Zondervan, 2005. p. 61.

15   Myra and Shelley, pp. 55-57.

16   Myra and Shelley, p. 59. Italics theirs.

17   McKee, John. "The Executive Suite Is Not So Sweet," Tech Decision Maker (Blog), August 11, 2010. https://www.techrepublic.com/blog/tech-decision-maker/the-executive-suite-is-not-so-sweet/. Accessed 2-9-21.

18   Cogan, Mordechai. *The Raging Torrent*. 2016. 14-19.

19   Noah Wiener, Tel Rehov *House Associated with the Biblical Prophet Elisha, Bible and archaeology news*, July 23, 2013, Biblical Archaeology Society, accessed 13 July 2019

20   Bean, Adam L., Christopher A. Rollston, P. Kyle McCarter, and Stefan J. Wimmer. 2018. "An Inscribed Altar from the Khirbat Ataruz Moabite Sanctuary". Levant. 50, no. 2: 211-236.

21   Lemaire, André. 2007. "The Mesha Stele and the Omri Dynasty". Library of Hebrew Old Testament Studies. no. 421: 135-144.

22   Manassa, Colleen. *The Great Karnak Inscription of Merneptah: Grand Strategy in the 13th Century BC*. New Haven: Conn, 2003.; Day, John. Molech: *A God of Human Sacrifice in the Old Testament*. Cambridge: Cambridge University Press, 1989.

23   Vaill, Peter B. *Managing as a Performing Art*. San Francisco, CA: Jossey-Bass Publishers, 1991.

24   Vaill, Peter B. *Learning as a Way of Being*. San Francisco, CA: Jossey-Bass Publishers, 1996.

25   Hagelia, Hallvard. *The Dan Debate: The Tel Dan Inscription in Recent Research*. Sheffield: Sheffield Phoenix Press, 2009.

26   Ephal, Israel, and Joseph Naveh. 1989. "Hazael's Booty Inscriptions". Israel Exploration Journal. 39, no. 3-4: 192-200;

Hasegawa, Shuichi. Aram and Israel during the Jehuite Dynasty. Berlin: De Gruyter, 2012.

27   Kuan, Jeffrey Kah-jin. *Neo-Assyrian Historical Inscriptions and Syria-Palestine: Israelite/Judean-Tyrian-Damascene Political and Commercial Relations in the Ninth-Eighth Century BCE.* 2016. 64-66.

28   Green, Alberto Ravinel Whitney. *The Role of Human Sacrifice in the Ancient Near East.* Ann Arbor, Michigan: University Microfilms International, 1984.

29   Free, Cathy. "Boy, 5, Steals Family Car…," The Washington Post, May 11, 2020. https://www.washingtonpost.com/ lifestyle/2020/05/11/boy-5-steals-family-car-attempt-buy-lamborghini-then-man-with-lamborghini-shows-up-his-house/. Accessed 09/08/2020

30   Malphurs, Aubrey, & Mancini, Will. *Building Leaders.* Grand Rapids, MI: Baker Books, 2004.

31   Malphurs and Mancini, p. 68.

32   Malphurs and Mancini, p. 70.

33   Malphurs and Mancini, pp. 70-71.

34   Both scholarly journals and popular press articles contain much information related to the Theory X and Theory Y theory concepts. For a general overview of the conversation, one may want to access this trade-related article: Forsch, Bill, and John Case. "The Challenge of Being a Theory Y Manager," Forbes Magazine, July 11, 2107. https://www.forbes.com/sites/fotschcase/2017/07/11/the-challenge-of-theory-y/#10bf4b3b42da. Accessed 09/10/20.

35   Livingston, J. Sterling. "Pygmalion in Management," Harvard Business Review, January 2003. https://hbr.org/2003/01/pygmalion-in-management. Accessed 09/10/2020

36   Shea, William H. 1978. "Adad-Nirari III and Jehoash of Israel". Journal of Cuneiform Studies. 30, no. 2: 101-113.

37   Swoboda, A.J. Subversive Sabbath. Ada, MI: Brazos Press, 2018. 7.

38   I often, as a quasi-joke, tell pastors that I have read many versions of the Bible and have never found one that puts an asterisk (*) by the fourth commandment with the note below saying "This day-a-week-for-rest" applies to everyone but fulltime ministers… these are allowed to work 24/7 until they crumble from mental, physical,

and emotional exhaustion and end up in as a straight-jacket singing 'Jesus love me this I know'"

39   I was exposed to these three disciplines of rest from Pastor Warren quite several years ago. Unfortunately, I did not note the media source at that time and do not remember the exact means from which he shared this information. Nonetheless, a quick Google search will reveal numerous sources where his model of "divert daily; withdraw weekly; abandon annually" can be accessed.

40   Pritchard, James B. *The Ancient Near East: Supplementary Texts and Pictures Relating to the Old Testament: Consisting of Supplementary Materials for The Ancient Near East in Pictures and Ancient Near Eastern Texts.* Princeton, New Jersey: Princeton University Press, 1969. 279-280.

41   Pritchard, James B. *The Ancient Near East in Pictures: Relating to the Old Testament.* Princeton: Princeton University Press, 1954. 120-122.

42   Mykytiuk, Lawrence J. Identifying Biblical Persons in Northwest Semitic Inscriptions of 1200-539 B.C.E. Atlanta: Society of Biblical Literature, 2004. 153-159.

43   Steven A. Austin, Gordon W. Franz, and Eric G. Frost, "Amos's Earthquake: An Extraordinary Middle East Seismic Event of 750 B.C." International Geology Review 42 (2000) 657-671.

44   Millard, A. R. *Reading, and Writing in the Time of Jesus.* Sheffield, England: Sheffield Academic Press, 2001.

45   Several of the elections and decisions mentioned will most likely be over by the time you read this. However, these only represent present examples in the ongoing debate and increasingly controversial climate that accompanies leadership transitions. We will all experience many more to come in the future!

46   Mykytiuk, Lawrence J. *Identifying Biblical Persons in Northwest Semitic Inscriptions of 1200-539 B.C.E.* Leiden: Brill, 2004. 27-31.

47   Deutsch, R. 1998. "First Impression - What We Learn from King Ahaz's Seal". Biblical Archaeology Review. 24, no. 3: 54-62.

48   Boardman, John; et al., eds. (1991). *The Cambridge Ancient History: The Assyrian and Babylonian Empires and Other States of the Near East, from the Eighth to the Sixth Centuries B.C. Vol. III.2.* Cambridge University Press. p. 336.

49   Burnett, Joel and Gharib, Romel. "The Amman Theatre Statue and the Ammonite Royall Ancestor Cult," ASOR: the American Schools of Oriental Research, December 2019. Accessed June 9, 2020. http://www.asor.org/anetoday/2019/12/Amman-Theatre-Statue-and-Ammonite-Royal-Ancestor-Cult

50   James B. Pritchard, ed., *Ancient Near Eastern Texts Relating to the Old Testament (3rd ed)*.; Princeton NJ: Princeton University Press, 1969) 283.

51   Tadmor, Hayim, Shigeo Yamada, and Jamie R. Novotny. *The Royal Inscriptions of Tiglath-Pileser III (744-727 BC) and Shalmaneser V (726-722 BC), Kings of Assyria*. Winona Lake, Ind: Eisenbrauns, 2011. 122.

52   Graham, Billy. "A Time for Moral Courage." The Virgin Islands Daily News. October 29, 1964. Reprinted by permission from Reader's Digest, July 1964. https://news.google.com/newspapers?nid=757&dat=19641029&id=rIcwAAAAIBAJ&sjid=lEQDAAAAIBAJ&pg=6379,1764784. Accessed 11/23/20.

53   Reardon, Kathleen K. "Courage as a Skill." Harvard Business Review. January 2007. https://hbr.org/2007/01/courage-as-a-skill Accessed 11/14/20.

54   Detert, James. "Cultivating Everyday Courage." Harvard Business Review. November 1, 2018. https://hbr.org/2018/11/cultivating-everyday-courage. Accessed 11/16/20. Italics his.

55   Goldberg, Melanie. "The Six Attributes of Courage." Psychology Today, August 23, 2012. https://www.psychologytoday.com/us/blog/the-mindful-self-express/201208/the-six-attributes-courage. Accessed 11/18/20. Parenthetical statements mine.

56   Levy, Lynne. Courage at Work: Lessons from Brené Brown. Overview of a talk given by Ms. Brown at Workhuman 2019 in Nashville, TN. https://www.workhuman.com/resources/globoforce-blog/courage-at-work-lessons-from-brené-brown# Accessed 11/15/20

57   Thanks to Andy Stanley and his insights in the 1997 book entitled *Like a Rock*. This definition of courage is adapted from his discussion in that book on character development.

58   These three principles, exemplified in a biblical leader, are found in Joseph's story (Gen. 37-50). Joseph certainly was "bitten" many times but was willing to allow God's difficult experiences and

process to refine and develop the courage to "get back in" when the opportunity of Divine destiny arose!

59   Meyer, F. B. *Joshua, and the Land of Promise.* Fort Washington, PA: Christian Literature Crusade, 1977.

60   Universiṭah ha-'Ivrit bi-Yerushalayim. Impression of King Hezekiah's Royal Seal Discovered in Ophel Excavations South of Temple Mount in Jerusalem. Jerusalem: The Hebrew University of Jerusalem, 2015.

61   Hallo, William W., and K. Lawson Younger. *Context of Scripture.* Leiden: Brill, 2003. 2. 119D.

62   James B. Pritchard, ed., *Ancient Near Eastern Texts Relating to the Old Testament (3rd ed.)*; Princeton NJ: Princeton University Press, 1969) 321.

63   Gallagher, William R. *Sennacherib's Campaign to Judah: New Studies.* 1999.

64   Herodotus, and W. G. Waddell. Herodotus, book II. London: Bristol Classical Press, 1998. 141.

65   Parpola, Simo. *The Murderer of Sennacherib.* [Copenhagen]: [Akademisk Forlag], 1980. 171-182.

66   Mazar, Eilat. "Is This the "Prophet Isaiah's Signature?" Biblical Archaeology Review 44:2, May/June 2018.

67   Biblical Archaeology Society Staff, "Hezekiah's Tunnel Reexamined." Biblical Archaeology Society, February 15, 2020. https://www.biblicalarchaeology.org/daily/biblical-sites-places/ jerusalem/hezekiahs-tunnel-reexamined. Accessed 10/1/20.

68   Aren Maeir, and Jeffrey Chadwick, "Regarding Recent Suggestions Redating the Siloam Tunnel." Biblical Archaeology Society, August 26, 2013. https://www.biblicalarchaeology.org/daily/biblical-sites-places/jerusalem/regarding-recent-suggestions-redating-the-siloam-tunnel. Accessed 10/3/20.

69   Avigad, N. 1963. "A Seal of 'Manasseh Son of the King'". Israel Exploration Journal. 13, no. 2: 133-136.

70   Pritchard, James B. *The Ancient Near East: Supplementary Texts and Pictures Relating to the Old Testament : Consisting of Supplementary Materials for The Ancient Near East in Pictures and Ancient Near Eastern Texts.* Princeton, New Jersey: Princeton University Press, 1969. 290-291.

71   Pritchard, James B. *The Ancient Near East: Supplementary Texts and Pictures Relating to the Old Testament : Consisting of Supplementary Materials for The Ancient Near East in Pictures and Ancient Near Eastern Texts.* Princeton, New Jersey: Princeton University Press, 1969. 294.

72   Rudman, Dominic. 2000. "A Note on the Personal Name Amon (2 Kings 21,19-26 II 2 Chr. 33,21-25)". Biblica. 81, no. 3: 403-405.

73   Ryholt, Kim (2004). "The Assyrian Invasion of Egypt in Egyptian Literary Tradition". In Dercksen, J.G. (ed.). Assyria and Beyond: Studies Presented to Mogens Trolle Larsen. Leiden: Nederlands Instituut voor het Nabije Oosten. pp. 483–510.

74   MacGinnis, J. D. A. (1988). "Ctesias and the Fall of Nineveh". Illinois Classical Studies. University of Illinois Press. 13 (1): 37–42.

75   Strong's Concordance. https://www.blueletterbible.org/lang/lexicon/lexicon.cfm?Strongs=H4519&t=NKJV. Accessed 1-10-2021.

76   Strong's Concordance. https://www.blueletterbible.org/lang/lexicon/lexicon.cfm?Strongs=H8582&t=NKJV. Accessed 1-29-21.

77   Merriam-Webster Dictionary. https://www.merriam-webster.com/dictionary/syncretism. Accessed 1-19-21.

78   Roosevelt, Theodore. Man in the Arena. Delivered April 23, 1910. Paris, France. http://www.worldfuturefund.org/Documents/maninarena.html. Full text accessed 1-18-21.

79   Weiss, Bari. "The Story Behind a 2,600-Year-Old Seal: Who was Nathan-Melech, the king's servant?" New York Times. March 30, 2019

80   James B. Pritchard, ed., Ancient Near Eastern Texts Relating to the Old Testament(3rd ed.; Princeton NJ: Princeton University Press, 1969) 568.

81   Yair Shoham, "Hebrew Bullae" in City of David Excavations: Final Report VI, Qedem 41 (Jerusalem: Hebrew University of Jerusalem, 2000), 33.

82   This definition is my compilation of the main components of the dictionary terms.

83   For more information, visit https://www.melfisher.org/.

84   *Forecastle Treasures. The Atocha History.* https://atocha.com/index.php?route=information/information&information_id=13. Accessed November 1, 2020.

85 Avigad, Nahman. 1979. "Baruch the Scribe and Jerahmeel the King's Son". The Biblical Archaeologist. 42, no. 2: 114-118.

86 Fant, Clyde E., and Mitchell Glenn Reddish. Lost Treasures of the Bible: Understanding the Bible Through Archaeological Artifacts in World Museums. Grand Rapids, MI: William B. Eerdmans Pub. Co, 2008. 218.

87 Arnold, Bill T., and Bryan Beyer. Readings from the Ancient Near East: Primary Sources for Old Testament Study. Grand Rapids, MI: Baker Academic, 2004. 159.

88 Hughes, Jeremy. *Secrets of the Times: Myth and History in Biblical Chronology.* Sheffield: Sheffield Academic Press, 1990. 229. This 1990 study listed eleven scholars who preferred 587 and eleven who preferred 586.

89 Kouzes, James, and Barry Posner. *The Leadership Challenge, 6th ed.* San Francisco: Jossey-Bass, 2017.

90 Kouzes, James, and Barry Posner. *Credibility: How Leaders Gain and Lose It, Why People Demand It, 2nd ed.* San Francisco: Jossey-Bass, 2011.

91 "Sensory Conflict Theory" overview. Oxford Reference. https://www.oxfordreference.com/view/10.1093/oi/authority.20110803100454911. Accessed 08/20/20

92 Wallis, David. "The Word on…Motion Sickness," The Washington Post, May 2, 1999, https://www.washingtonpost.com/archive/lifestyle/travel/1999/05/02/the-word-on-motion-sickness/a10a6301-1eea-49a7-9ce0-d4dba81f1355/. Accessed 08/21/20

93 *Strong's Concordance.* Reference G1374. https://www.blueletterbible.org/lang/Lexicon/Lexicon.cfm?strongs=G1374&t=KJV